AF322842

Pioneer of the Chinese Revolution

Zhang Binglin and Confucianism

Pioneer of
the Chinese Revolution

Zhang Binglin and Confucianism

SHIMADA KENJI

Translated by Joshua A. Fogel

Stanford University Press
Stanford, California
1990

"Zhang Binglin: Traditional Chinese Scholar and Revolutionary" was originally published as "Shō Heirin ni tsuite: Chūgoku dentō gakujutsu to kakumei," in Shimada Kenji, *Chūgoku kakumei no senkushatachi* (Pioneers of the Chinese Revolution) (Tokyo: Chikuma shobō, 1970), pp. 167–271; "Confucius in the Era of the 1911 Revolution" was originally published as "Shingai kakumei ki no Kōshi mondai," in *Shingai kakumei no kenkyū* (Studies in the 1911 Revolution), ed. Onogawa Hidemi and Shimada Kenji (Tokyo: Chikuma shobō, 1978), pp. 3–35. Translated by permission of the author.

Stanford University Press
Stanford, California
© 1990 by the Board of Trustees
of the Leland Stanford Junior University
Printed in the United States of America

CIP data are at the end of the book

CONTENTS

INTRODUCTION

Shimada Kenji's Contributions to the Study of East Asian History

One senses when one begins reading virtually anything written by Shimada Kenji, Professor Emeritus of East Asian History at Kyoto University, that one has entered a realm where a great mind is at work. Old ideas begin to take on new meanings, and new ideas and new approaches to familiar themes unsettle the reader's thoughts. It all seems so novel and yet so clear.

Most of Shimada's career has been tied to Kyoto University. He received his undergraduate degree there in 1941, and beginning in 1949 he was Associate Professor at the Research Institute of Humanistic Sciences, moving over to the Faculty of Letters some years later. Before retiring in 1977, he lectured and led seminars on everything from ancient Chinese thought to Neo-Confucianism in China and Japan, to Sino-Japanese relations in the late nineteenth century, to the history of the Chinese Revolution.

Unlike many other Japanese Sinologists and Japanologists, Shimada has not produced an enormous corpus of writings, published and republished in countless ways. He has written three books, edited and translated about a dozen others, and published a fair number of articles and a modest number of reviews. A brief overview just of his book-length contributions to the field will suffice to convey the breadth of his work.

Many argue that his first book, derived from his college thesis, is still his most influential piece of work: *Chūgoku ni okeru kindai shii no zasetsu* (The frustration of modern thought in China) (Tokyo: Chikuma shobō, 1949; reissue, 1970). This book effectively opened the field of Ming thought to serious scholarship in Japan and abroad. As Shimada noted in his introduction, most scholars had been content until then to see the intellectualism of the Qing as derivative of trends in the Song, but had failed to find intellectual depth in the intervening centuries under the Ming. In fact, most had adopted the early Qing thinkers' bias against Ming thought as egotistic and ultimately destructive.

Shimada argued that there was real intellectual substance to many thinkers of the Ming era, principally Wang Yangming (1472–1528), his followers, and Li Zhi (1527–1602). These men were not merely outlandish iconoclasts, as their detractors claimed, but serious thinkers who drew their inspiration from the same corpus of classical and "modern" writings as their more respected intellectual opponents. Shimada demonstrated that, far from representing a wholesale rejection of Song thought and learning, the thinkers of the Ming period owed their roots precisely to the Song and its rootedness in classical antiquity. What differed were the emphases, not the sources. By situating Ming thinkers, and especially the self-avowed iconoclast Li Zhi, in this filiation, Shimada successfully reintegrated Chinese intellectual history, although his views were not immediately accepted.

Shimada's second book, *Shushigaku to Yōmeigaku* (The Zhu Xi school and the Wang Yangming school) (Tokyo: Iwanami shoten, 1967), continued these themes, albeit with a sharper focus. It demonstrated, among other things, the profound and intrinsic links between the schools of these two most celebrated thinkers in Chinese history, one of the Song and the other of the Ming. This effort flew in the face of the long-standing practice of bifurcating Chinese thought of the Song, Yuan, and Ming periods into Zhu and Wang schools. If we have all now moved in a similar direction, it is largely due to Shimada's pioneering work and its influence on the writings of Wm. Theodore deBary, Wing-tsit Chan, and Tu Wei-ming, among others, in the West.

Shimada's third book appeared just a few years ago, *Shin juka tetsugaku ni tsuite: Yū Jūriki no tetsugaku* (On the philosophy of a Neo-Confucian: The philosophy of Xiong Shili) (Kyoto: Dōhōsha, 1987), a monograph on a "Neo-Confucian" thinker in the People's Republic of China, Xiong Shili (1885–1968). After placing Xiong in the context of the May Fourth generation and the subsequent revival of Confucianism, Shimada compared his work to that of his slightly younger contemporary, Feng Youlan (b. 1895). Fully a third of this book, though, is a close textual analysis of Xiong's major work, *Xin Weishi lun* (On a new consciousness-only philosophy).

In addition, Shimada participated in the editing of various works by Ogyū Sorai, Wang Yangming, and Nakae Chōmin. He also recently served as general editor of the five-volume *Ajia rekishi kenkyū nyūmon* (Introduction to the study of Asian history) (Kyoto: Dōhōsha, 1983–   ). In individual essays, he has addressed the work of Wang Gen, Tan Sitong, Zhang Binglin, Li Zhi, Zhang Xuecheng, Yang Cihu, Gong Zizhen, Miura Baien, Yokoi Shōnan, Nakae Chōmin, and Miyazaki Tōten. His translations from Chinese include an annotated edition of *The Great Learning* and *The Doctrine of the Mean*, as well as writings by Liang Qichao, Chen Tianhua, Zou Rong, Sun Zhongshan, Tan Sitong, Zhang Binglin, and Kang Youwei.

Thus, the two essays translated here are selections from that part of Shimada's larger corpus that concerns the late imperial period. At the same time, they also convey much of the richness of his work and provide an excellent point of entry into this corpus. These two essays both touch on one of his abiding themes, the influence of domestic Chinese systems of thought on the development of Chinese revolutionary thought. Shimada would never deny the importance of foreign, non–East Asian influences on the Chinese Revolution, but he clearly minimizes them in relation to native forces. To undertake the massive project of laying out the native Chinese intellectual influences on revolutionary Chinese thought, one must be conversant with the entire sweep of Chinese intellectual history. One cannot simply ignore "traditional" thought as an epiphenomenon or rely on a catechism of several stock ideas about the past in analyzing the emergence and growth of Chinese revolutionary thought. Here we see Shimada's greatest strength, a profound knowledge of the history of Chinese philosophy and religion brought to bear on the people and ideas that culminated in the 1911 Revolution and the end of the imperial institution in China. Shimada takes his modern subjects with complete seriousness when they drew on "traditional" ideas from their own history to justify radical change in the late nineteenth and early twentieth centuries.

Shimada's approach clashes sharply with another trend, much more pervasive in scholarly circles in China, the West, and even Japan—namely, an inability to understand any phenomenon that appears to fall simultaneously into two allegedly opposing structures. In other words, the dogmatism of contemporary scholars and our categories of analysis have inhibited our understanding of modern Chinese history, because we have been unable to arrive at categories either large enough or flexible enough for the subject. For example, until Shimada's work on Zhang Binglin (and long after it as well), Zhang was *never*, not once, critically assessed as a whole person. The inability to place him in either the "traditional" or the "modern" camp (in Marxist circles, the dichotomy was usually between "feudal" and "progressive") meant either that Zhang had to be seen as going through two or more separable phases (from "traditional" to "modern" and then backsliding late in life to his essentially "traditional" self), or that he had to be dismissed as a crackpot, albeit a brilliant one.

Shimada's path-breaking piece on Zhang debunks this myth right at the start. Zhang, he argues, is both a traditional scholar and a revolutionary. The question then is not how these two sides of his character continually conflict, with one occasionally gaining ascendancy over the other, but how in Zhang's own understanding each facet *necessitated* the other. Shimada eschews the usual wonderment that such an apparently intelligent man was unable to take the one "obvious" step of dispensing with the silly trappings of "tradition" and step into the "modern" age with both feet. By turning the structure of received analysis on its head, Shimada presents in Zhang Binglin a whole person for whom no apologies are needed, no explanations about an emotional commitment to a discredited past in conflict with the obvious facts of the modern Western world.

Shimada's analytic style has always been to take the ideas of his research subjects seriously in and of themselves; not to look for an extraneous "reason" why a particular thinker had to come to a particular conclusion that may look bizarre to us today. He does not conflate the entire history of late-Qing intellectual trends into a Manichean struggle between the perverse forces of "tradition" and the advancing forces of "modernity." Indeed, he sees tradition as a multitude of streams of thought, some brought to serve the cause of revolution (culminating in 1911), others employed to attack it. Confucian Chinese scholarship and anti-Westernism need not, in Shimada's work, imply an automatic aversion to the Republican revolutionary movement. This point will be made in a variety of ways in the essays that follow, as Shimada addresses topics ranging from the revival of *zhuzi* studies in the *kaozheng* or evidential research movement of the eighteenth century to the importance of late-Qing Buddhist scholarship.

The central figure of the two essays and the principal subject of the longer of them is Zhang Binglin, possibly the most misunderstood person in the late-Qing revolutionary movement. Shimada aims at explaining how Zhang himself saw the inextricable linkage between a wholehearted devotion to traditional Chinese scholarship—indeed, the very preservation of that tradition—and the anti-Manchu revolutionary cause. Often dismissed as a crackpot, brilliant or otherwise, or as a perverse intransigent incapable of comprehending the modern world as it passed him by, Zhang has never received the kind of attention in the West that his importance to his own era earns him.

Even when he has been accorded the courtesy of sympathetic scholarly attention, Zhang's intellectual depths have not been fully plumbed, in large part because his work is so difficult to read—it is indeed forbidding, if not altogether impenetrable. The contemporary critic of Zhang's work must have extraordinary training in "traditional" Chinese materials and an uncommon command of classical Chinese sources. These are not the traditional strengths of scholars of the 1911 Revolution.

Scholarly writing on Zhang abounds in the People's Republic of China (PRC), outstripping in quantitative terms work on any other figure of the period except possibly Sun Zhongshan. Although more sophisticated work appeared in the late 1980's in China, as a whole Chinese scholarship has been marred by an overwhelming concern to see all intellectual history as a conflict between materialism (the normative "good") and idealism (the normative "evil"); and by the concomitant tendency to bisect

Zhang into "progressive" and "regressive" halves. Even when reasonably thorough analyses of one or another aspect of Zhang's life and writing occupy center stage in such work, the final result is doomed to failure, as is any attempt to understand Zhang's intellectual efforts as a bipolar struggle between tradition and modernity. Zhang's work is too complex and rich to afford such a conclusion, as Shimada demonstrates.

The second of the essays translated here deals with an issue that has never received concerted attention anywhere else so far as I know. How could the figure of Confucius have been deified by the leaders of the 1898 Reform Movement and then, less than two decades later, be excoriated by the leaders of the May Fourth Movement? What happened to cause the precipitous decline in the fortunes of "Confucius and Sons"? Shimada analyzes the views of Confucius and Confucianism of all the major groups (including the Qing government and overseas Chinese in Europe) in the period under study (1895–1919) before suggesting some answers to this fascinating query. Among the issues he deals with here are the acrimonious debates over whether China should adopt a "national religion" and, if so, what it should be. Once again, although Shimada clearly betrays a preference for the likes of Zhang Binglin in his vituperative debate with Kang Youwei and the advocates of a Confucian religion, the latter receive equal time and their endeavors are considered with full seriousness.

To the extent that Shimada's work is known in the West, it has been through his writings on Neo-Confucianism in China and Japan. Reference to those writings will be found throughout the text and in notes to the many path-breaking conference volumes edited by Wm. Theodore deBary and others over the past twenty years. In many ways, the first of these volumes, *Self and Society in Ming Thought* (New York: Columbia University Press, 1970), attempted to redress the balance with which Shimada had been concerned in his first book-length work. The essays in *Self and Society* represented a group effort both to take the thinkers of the Ming seriously and to see them as part of a longer tradition of Chinese thought. The nuances, approaches, and emphases in deBary's own magisterial essay in that volume, "Individualism and Humanitarianism in Late Ming Thought" (pp. 145–245), owes much to Shimada's pioneering work, and it speaks volumes for the lasting import of ideas generated in the Ming for the late-Qing radical cause.

It was in part because I find Shimada's work so compelling and in part because my own speciality lies in the later period covered by the two essays translated here that I chose them. Although considerable work has been done on Zhang Binglin since Shimada's essay first appeared, the essay has achieved classic status in Japan and was certainly the impetus to other work that followed; and it has never been superseded. The second essay is in many ways even more thought-provoking. The subject is so obvious a major theme in modern Chinese intellectual history that one wonders why it was never discussed before Shimada. It may yet spawn a series of debates.

J.A.F.

ONE

Zhang Binglin:
Traditional Chinese Scholar
and Revolutionary

For the term "traditional scholarship," I might just as well have used "traditional thought." Furthermore, "revolution" in the sense I mean here refers to the 1911 Revolution in China. When scholars speak of traditional Chinese thought, they generally mean the three schools of Confucianism, Buddhism, and Daoism. Hence my intention here will be to examine the links between the 1911 Revolution and Confucian, Buddhist, and Daoist ideas. I will be seeking answers to questions such as: Which of these three forged bonds with the revolution? Which contributed to the revolution? I want to do this by looking particularly at the case of Zhang Binglin (1869–1936).

Schools of Chinese Thought and Zhang's Place as Heir to Them

I pick Zhang Binglin (or Zhang Taiyan) because, among the leaders of the 1911 Revolution, scarcely anyone other than Sun Zhongshan (Sun Yat-sen, 1866–1925) is well-known outside China. By examining Zhang, we will be better able to understand the import of the 1911 Revolution within the totality of Chinese intellectual history. The reason I chose "traditional *scholarship*" and not "traditional *thought*" is that the former is more appropriate in a study that centers on Zhang. As concerns the term "revolution"—the opposition between it and reform (radical reform, constitutional monarchism) became ever so clear later; but it should be understood that in the period under discussion, revolution and reform tended to be used in a way that nebulously linked them, for revolution tended to subsume reform.

Which of the systems of ideas within "traditional Chinese thought" actively contributed to revolution? One of my conclusions will be that we must exclude Daoism from the list. In other words, only Confucianism and Buddhism qualify here. Although Daoism was the most closely tied to the lives of the common people, one cannot really point to any contribution it made toward revolution. By my theory about how one should count traditional systems of Chinese thought, in addition to Confucianism, Buddhism, and Daoism, which always come up, it is important to add to this list one more: the schools of the *zhuzi* thinkers, those noncanonical schools of Chinese thought in the pre-Han era. Including these thinkers complicates the problem a bit, but it does not alter the conclusion. Of course the role played, for example, by secret societies in the revolutionary movement was considerable, and as can be clearly seen in the initiation ceremonies for new members in some of them, numerous Daoist elements were adopted. I would argue, however, that one cannot conclude from this that secret societies took shape and operated on the basis of Daoist thought.

Furthermore, the groups responsible for "peasant uprisings" ever since the Yellow Turban rebellion late in the second century C.E. (at the end of the Later Han dynasty) have in many cases been bound by Daoist belief systems. Despite the recent inclination to point to such instances of rebellion as harbingers of revolution, for our purposes we need not consider them together. When we examine the speeches and activities of the revolutionary thinkers at the time of the 1911 Revolution and the slogans adopted at the time by the popular movement, nothing is identifiable as being based in Daoist thought. Also, I know of no Daoist, Daoist monk, or anyone close to that rank who was active in the revolution. Perhaps the incompatibility of Daoism and "revolution" is best illustrated by the Boxer Uprising. The Boxers were "Daoists," closely linked with the daily travails of the common people, and extraordinarily superstitious.

Thus my current view is that of the three schools of thought, only Confucianism and Buddhism were actively at work at the time of the revolution. "Confucianism and Buddhism" is quite a mouthful, for there have been numerous schools of both. I think it would be useful at this point to describe this multiplicity of schools *to the extent necessary for the work that follows.*

Confucianism divides first into philosophy (the study of nature, principle, and the like) and documentary research (evidential, bibliographic studies, and the like). "Philosophy" refers here to Song learning as represented by the school of its foremost proponent, Zhu Xi (1130–1200), and the Lu-Wang school (named for Lu Xiangshan, 1139–92 of the Song, and Wang Yangming, 1472–1528 of the Ming), which opposed the Zhu Xi school, both of which have long been well-known. In addition, "philosophy" includes the philosophy of Zhang Zai (1020–77), one of Zhu Xi's forerunners and a member of the Song school in the broader sense, whose views might stand like a tripod along with those of the Zhu Xi and Lu-Wang schools. This division of schools approximates the one recently articulated by scholars in the PRC. In fact, Zhang Zai's thought was absorbed by Zhu Xi and his followers, and it was not passed down as a school of its own.

Nonetheless, in the late Ming and early Qing eras, the great philosopher Wang Fuzhi (1619–92) revived Zhang's views; and on the eve of the revolution in our century, Tan Sitong (1865–98), who is better seen as a revolutionary than as a reformer, became fascinated by Wang Fuzhi's philosophy. Thus, when we construct the problem in this way, in terms of influence on the 1911 Revolution, it becomes appropriate to list all three as founders of philosophical schools: Zhu Xi, Lu-Wang, and Zhang Zai. For present purposes, the three can represent Confucian philosophy: Zhang Zai's so-called materialism, with priority placed on *qi* ("ether," or a kind of metaphysical matter); Zhu Xi's so-called objective materialism, with priority placed on *li* ("principle"); and the Lu-Wang school's "subjective materialism," with priority placed on "heart and mind" (*xin*). (We should probably add the distinctive philosophy of history of the Gongyang or New Text school, but for convenience, I will include this school in the later discussion of "documentary research.")

In opposition to what we have referred to as philosophy, "documentary research" or evidential scholarship (*kaozhengxue*) arose in the Qing and branded the former empty speculation. Evidential scholarship was originally a methodology for examination of the classics, as in the work of one of its founders, Gu Yanwu

(1613–82), and its proponents evinced little interest in events of the day. In this respect it was ultimately no different from Song and Ming philosophy, which aimed at organizing the state and bringing peace to the world. Descending into *kaozhengxue* based simply on "seeking truth on the basis of facts" and showing a marked aversion to current events were due to the extraordinary thoroughness of the Qing state's repressive policies.

Various ways of subdividing *kaozhengxue* into its major branches have been tried, but for the purposes of this study I would like to divide it into the following five components: classical studies, particularly research based on philology and phonology; historical studies; studies of ritual systems; New Text scholarship (namely, the Gongyang school); and *zhuzi* studies.

The first of these, philological exegesis (often called *xiaoxue* in Chinese), was essentially the study of the Chinese language. It has become a well-established view that this domain produced the most outstanding results within *kaozhengxue* in the Qing period. Zhang Binglin was a scholar who truly carried on the orthodox tradition of philology within *kaozhengxue*, and he was also a revolutionary.

The second subdivision, historical studies, meant primarily textual criticism of historical writings (geography was traditionally considered part of history), not simply historiography. We should also note that remarkable scholars like Zhang Xuecheng (1738–1801) emerged within the area of historical theory and established what might be called a philosophy of *kaozhengxue*, which was at the same time a philosophy that transcended (in the Hegelian sense) *kaozhengxue*. Zhang Xuecheng's theories exerted an enormous influence on the advocates of "national learning" (*guoxue*) during the period of the 1911 Revolution, notably on Zhang Binglin.

Studies of ritual institutions and systems were based on documentary work and were thoroughly empirical, so they fall within the arena of *kaozhengxue*. In fact, in the narrow sense, the examination of ritual systems insofar as they are described in the classics filled numerous works of a pure *kaozheng* sort. Conversely, studies of institutions over time that linked changes in ritual to the politics of the time were somewhat different in nature from *kaozhengxue*. This point deserves a bit more attention. The most evident characteristic of *kaozhengxue* was the fact that the entirety of Qing scholarship was held in restraint, with studies of ritual institutions being one established part of *kaozhengxue*. Perhaps it would be better to use the expression "empiricism" for cases, such as studies of ritual, in which one wants to convey a slightly different coloration than *kaozhengxue* would. Zhang Xuecheng's historiographical theories, which are usually contrasted with *kaozhengxue*, to this extent represent a Qing empiricist philosophy.

The fourth and fifth groupings under this general rubric include New Text research and *zhuzi* studies. These both emerged after the heyday of *kaozhengxue*. They were like offspring born in spite of themselves to parents they did not resemble. Let us first look at the New Text school. The original aim of New Text scholars was to offer an explanation of the Confucian classical texts, in a manner consistent with the historical era from which those texts hailed—immediately after the book burning ordered by the founder of the Qin dynasty, Qin Shi Huangdi (r. 221–10 B.C.E.). These texts, including such works as *Gongyang zhuan* (Gongyang Commentary [on the *Chunqiu* or *Spring and Autumn Annals*]), which had been written in the "new script," the popular form for Chinese characters at that time, were used in the curriculum of the national university during the Former Han dynasty. Stimulated by the essence of *kaozhengxue* to press ever further back in time for classical authority, the New Text movement pushed one step beyond the tide of earlier *kaozhengxue*, which had fastened on Later Han classical research as a scholarly pinnacle.

New Text classicism in the Former Han embodied, in a word, classical scholarship for utilitarian purposes, and in this respect it clearly differed from the scholasticism of Qing *kaozhengxue*. Furthermore, the gist of the classical work central to the New Text movement, the *Gongyang Commentary*, argued for examining the "subtle words and great meaning" (*weiyan dayi*) contained in Confucius's *Spring and Autumn Annals*; in other words, it called for examination of Confucius's philosophy of history, which, they argued, was a philosophy of reform. It would seem that *kaozhengxue* had spawned something conspicuously different from it, and in so doing it gave rise to a major disturbance. New Text reformist (in a sense later distinguished from revolutionary) thinkers such as Kang Youwei (1858–1927), Liang Qichao (1873–1929), and Tan Sitong, might originally have best been referred to as revolutionary thinkers. The greatest achievement of Zhang Binglin as a revolutionary was to begin the head-on struggle with reformism and, after assuming leadership in the struggle, to stand strong and to purify the principles of revolution.

Zhuzi studies were clearly a product of the *kaozhengxue* movement. *Zhuzi* is a short-hand expression for the so-called Hundred Schools, and often the terms are used together: *zhuzi baijia* (*zhuzi* and Hundred Schools). The term refers to a wide variety of scholars and thinkers who debated one another throughout China from the late Spring and Autumn period through the Warring States period at the end of the Zhou dynasty. These Hundred Schools have traditionally been divided into nine major branches: Confucians, Daoists, *yinyang* theorists, Legalists, logicians, Mohists, itinerant political theorists, miscellaneous scholars, and agriculturalists.

As this list indicates, Confucianism was originally just one of these nine branches. At the time of the famous Emperor Wu (r. 140–87 B.C.E.) of the Former Han, following an imperial order of 136 B.C.E., the other schools receded and only Confucian scholarship received public recognition for instruction in the national school system (texts at that time were in the new script, as described above). Later, the non-Confucian *zhuzi* schools rapidly died out, and, with a few exceptions, their scholarly traditions were effectively broken off. However, one should not conclude from this that the decline of *zhuzi* as schools meant that their texts—such as the Legalist work *Hanfeizi* or the Mohist text *Mozi*—disappeared or ceased being read for educational purposes. As schools the *zhuzi* disappeared, and eventually there were no thinkers who sought to base their theories on works representing *zhuzi* schools of thought. This situation continued through the Qing dynasty.

Possible exceptions to this general statement about the *zhuzi* schools are the classical Daoist texts, *Laozi* and *Zhuangzi*. In the first place, these texts were passed down as sacred Daoist scriptures. Second, and even more important, they never lacked for admirers throughout the ages among the general, non-Daoist intelligentsia. The first point might suggest that Daoists had maintained their existence as a school; however, as severely critical scholars have noted, the theories of Laozi and Zhuangzi differ markedly from later religious Daoism. As a popular religion, Daoism bore scarcely any relation to the ideas expressed in these two canonical texts, and the positions held by Laozi and Zhuangzi as Daoist divinities were by no means high. It was in a realm apart from popular Daoism that the intellectual side of Laozi and Zhuangzi was preserved—among admirers in the general scholar-official world (most of whom were tenacious Confucians). In a country like China, in which autocratic government and bureaucratic structure reached unprecedented heights at such a remarkably early stage, the Daoist classics provided indispensable comfort for a segment of the intellectual elite, for their own internal freedom.

Kaozhengxue of the Qing period was originally a sphere of learning that fell under the umbrella of Confucianism. That is to say, because evidentiary research on the "classics" was its main thread, even in cases where texts written by *zhuzi* scholars were cited in the broad search for evidence, ultimately these *zhuzi* texts were regarded every time simply as corroborative material. As the *kaozheng* movement proceeded, though, eventually scholars emerged who made these *zhuzi* texts their specialty. Although initially their studies did not depart from the philological and comparative textual mold of *kaozheng*, the next stage of research required them to examine the *zhuzi* writings as "thought." As the saying went, "There are disadvantages to attacking heterodoxy," and *zhuzi* studies, although not the object of research concerns on their own, ultimately were revived in this roundabout manner.

What happened when the undermining of traditional Confucian authority occasioned by the impact of the West met with such a trend in the scholarly world? In the discussion of the relationship between traditional Chinese thought and revolution above, I noted that what we designate as "traditional thought" should not just be the three conventionally listed schools of Confucianism, Buddhism, and Daoism, but that we need to add the *zhuzi* schools to the mix. It was this intellectual-historical background I had in mind when I pointed to the ideas of the various *zhuzi* scholars who were "rediscovered" in the Qing period. *Zhuzi* traditions were different from the transmissions of Confucian, Buddhist, and Daoist teachings, which were vibrant traditions, continually passed down throughout Chinese history. The regeneration of the *zhuzi* transpired entirely within one domain under the realm of the Confucian school.

On the eve of the 1911 Revolution, furthermore, Chinese intellectual history seems to have reverted to its origins. In the *Renxue* (On benevolence), that famous work in which Tan Sitong developed revolutionary ideas and a devastating critique of Confucianism, Tan professed two concepts taken from Mozi: *jian'ai* or universal love (widely recognized since the time of Mencius as a doctrine befitting only wild animals), and *xia* or the knight-errant.

We can now understand how Zhang Binglin came to advocate the teachings of the *zhuzi*. In his understanding of the *zhuzi* schools, Zhang restored Confucianism to its place as one of the original nine branches of classical learning and Confucius to his place as simply one scholar among the Hundred Schools. In this sense, I refer to Zhang's conception of *kaozhengxue* as "national learning." The Gongyang school, reformist in nature, had an international essence to its thought, was more positive in its evaluation of things European, and advocated a Confucian religion. By contrast, the revolutionary Zhang Binglin (who might well be described as a racialist) was thoroughly opposed to Confucianism as a religion. The trend to "doubt antiquity," which became a great scholarly issue in the Republican period, emerged primarily under the influence of the Gongyang reformers, and we should note from the outset that men of Zhang Binglin's ilk were generally indifferent to this antiquity-doubting.

We move now to examine the various schools of Buddhism. Once enormously popular, in the Sui and Tang, various philosophical sects—such as Sanlun, Tiantai, Huayan, and Weishi Buddhism—boasted speculative intensity, depth, rigor, force (in a good sense), and a wealth of human talent. European thinkers of this early period could not begin to compare. From the Song on, these schools generally lost vigor, while the Chan (Zen) and Pure Land sects took their place and became the most widespread. They too declined, and by the time of the Qing dynasty they displayed little religious energy or intellectuality to which one can point. If Buddhism had any recognition, it was not within the realm of doctrine, but among a small number of scholar-official believers, so-called lay Buddhists. From the early nineteenth century on in particular, one notes a large number of Gongyang (or New Text) scholars who were simultaneously followers of Buddhism. On the whole, though, Buddhism figured neither as a powerful undercurrent nor as a lively element in social thought of the time. Yet there was no period in which Buddhism was as broad an undercurrent as in the Qing.

Late in the Qing period, roughly the two decades preceding the 1911 Revolution, this situation changed radically, and Buddhism was revived. This development, like the rise of *zhuzi* studies, did not mark a revival within the religious world, but young intellectuals, particularly patriotic young men of derring-do, sought out Buddhism with enthusiasm. As Liang Qichao put it: "There was not a single late-Qing scholar of the 'new learning' who lacked ties to Buddhism." In this vein, the famous lay Buddhist Yang Wenhui (Yang Renshan, 1837–1911), published and circulated countless Buddhist texts of many different sects and devoted all his energies to the propagation of Buddhism. Yang was also a member of the enlightened young intelligentsia and had twice made trips to Europe. Furthermore, in terms of filiation, his work clearly belonged to the line of Buddhist studies undertaken by Gongyang advocates. Even so, it is startling that Buddhist studies undertaken by these radical young men at the end of the Qing were of the Huayan and Weishi varieties, particularly the latter, which was well-known for its thoroughgoing idealism and scholasticism.

The chief points in Zhang Binglin's idea of saving the nation with Buddhism were the role played by the bodhisattva in Huayan Buddhism and the philosophy of Weishi. Zhang himself pointed out that Weishi was by nature evidentiary, analytic, and thoroughly theoretical, and that it resembled *kaozhengxue* and science in this regard.[1] There is probably an even deeper reason as well. There were at least two scholars among the late-Ming patriots who amused themselves with Weishi Buddhism, men whom the late-Qing revolutionaries were wont to recall with profound emotion. One was the aforementioned Wang Fuzhi, author of *Xiangzong luosuo* (Guide to the Yogācāra [3 *juan*]) and *Sanzang fashi pashi guiju lun zan* (Encomium to the *Treatise on the Model of the Eight Consciousnesses* by Xuanzang); the other was the younger brother of Huang Zongxi (1610–95), Huang Zonghui (1616–63), author of *Yujia shidi lunzhu* (Commentary to the Yogācāra–bhūmi–śāstra [several thousand *juan*]) and *Cheng Weishi lunzhu* (Commentary on the *Treatise of the Completion of Weishi* [several thousand *juan*]).[2]

With the classification we have just used, which of the schools of Confucianism and Buddhism forged ties with the revolution and which did not? One answer is that the Zhu Xi school of Confucianism was unable to link up with the revolution. The Zhu Xi school was idealist, representing "objective idealism" in the language of PRC scholars. In this intellectual value-ranking, it has to be placed in a position beneath the *qi*-based philosophy of Zhang Zai and Wang Fuzhi, which has been deemed materialist. Nonetheless, the Zhu Xi school still stands a rung above the Lu-Wang school's "subjective idealism." This line of argument notwithstanding, insofar as thinkers from these schools contributed to the 1911 Revolution, the philosophies of Zhang Zai and Wang Fuzhi, for example, were inspirational for Tan Sitong; the Lu-

Traditional Chinese Thought

Zhuzi*†	Taoism	Buddhism		Confucianism
		Huayan*†	*kaozheng*	*philosophy*
		Weishi*†	*zhuzi* schools*†	Lu-Wang school*
		Pure Land	New Text school	Zhu Xi school
		Chan	(Gongyang)*	Zhang Zai / Wang
			Ritual studies†	Fuzhi*†
			Historical studies†	
			Classical studies†	

NOTE: Names with an * fall primarily within the fold of the reformist, Gongyang clique; those with a † are items connected to Zhang Binglin as revolutionary.

Wang school for Kang Youwei, Tan Sitong, Liang Qichao, and oddly enough, Liu Shipei (1884–1919), who was part of a *kaozheng* lineage; the *zhuzi* for Tan Sitong (*Mozi*), Liang Qichao (*Mozi*), and Zhang Binglin (the *zhuzi* generally and *Zhuangzi*, *Hanfeizi*, *Xunzi*, and *Mozi* in particular); and Buddhism for Kang Youwei, Tan Sitong, Liang Qichao, Zhang Binglin, Huang Zongyang (1865–1920), and others.

Even though each of these schools of thought played its role in the revolution (or radical reform), and even though broad knowledge in such areas as phonology, philology, and textual criticism was mobilized by Zhang Binglin to serve the revolutionary cause, only the Zhu Xi school seems not to have played any active part for the cause. The name Zhu Ciqi (1807–82), Kang Youwei's teacher from Jiujiang, does come faintly to mind, but Zhu Xi's influence is indirect at best.

It is not the intention of this essay to examine each and every one of the items sketched above. My aim is to examine Zhang Binglin as a "revolutionary" on the basis of the history of Chinese thought—Chinese intellectual history. It was as background to such an analysis of Zhang that this scheme was laid out. If this scheme could be put in schematic form, it would look like the diagram above.

Zhang's Political and Scholarly Activities

No one with any degree of interest in Chinese scholarship and thought is unaware of Zhang Binglin. As a disciple of the erudite scholar Yu Yue (1821–1906), Zhang continued the orthodox line of *kaozhengxue* in the Qing period. As a brilliant scholar, "the great master of national learning" (*guoxue dashi*) who transformed this orthodoxy into a "national learning," Zhang was also a passionate fighter for the Chinese Revolution who never retreated before the enemy. He was a ferocious polemicist, indeed an extraordinarily impulsive eccentric, who went so far as to adopt the alias of "maniac" (*fengzi*); once the revolution had been successful, he advocated reading the Confucian classics—only reading them, for he would have nothing to do with efforts to turn Confucianism into a religion. He opposed writing in the vernacular; he opposed study of the Shang oracle bones; he castigated the education offered in Chinese schools, castigated students, and castigated the new (i.e., European-style) learning; he attacked the Chinese Communist Party, and he ridiculed parliamentary government. Zhang is well-known as a perverse, obstinate man, opposed to virtually everything new.

It was Zhang Binglin who first formulated the name for China of "Zhonghua Minguo" (Republic of China). Zhang was the first to devise a national phonetic alphabet as the most effective means of eradicating illiteracy in China; and not only China itself, but those of us who study China, would one day be enormously grateful for this phonetic alphabet. Of the 37 elements of the phonetic alphabet now in use, 15 were adopted from Zhang's scheme. Among his more specialized, scholarly accomplishments, his originality in the field of phonology was positively brilliant. The ideas developed in his *Chengyun tu* (Outline of the Chengyun Dictionary) were refined further by his outstanding disciple Huang Kan (1886–1936) into the thesis of the 28 divisions of ancient rhymes; and this theory is now essentially the established view. For a time it was said that scholars in Beijing boasted of "our 28 divisions" of rhymes.

Zhang was of course not the first to argue the principle that research on the ancient Chinese language had to be based not so much on the written forms of characters, but on their sound, that is, on phonology. Yet we can count among his achievements the fact that he defended this idea his entire life and established innovative principles for others to follow; and in his later work on Chinese linguistics, he saw this as an expression of his "Chineseness." His work on Chinese dialectology ("Xin fangyan" or Modern dialects) was not merely a fanciful collection of materials; in linking it to the structure of his work on Chinese phonology, he effectively pioneered a new field of research.

Again, it was Zhang Binglin whose contributions in the history of philosophy went beyond mere philology and the writing of commentaries, for it was he who pioneered the field of "*zhuzi* studies" in the sense we use that term today. In this regard, the research of Hu Shi (1891–1962) on the history of ancient Chinese logic was an extension of the pioneering work of Zhang. Furthermore, Zhang drew attention to thinkers and scholars of the past who had generally been ignored, such as Tang Zhen (1630–1704) and Zhang Xuecheng, and he extolled the value of the *Mengzi ziyi shuzheng* (Exegesis of the meaning of terms in the *Mencius*) by Dai Zhen (1723–77). Dai Zhen's work would later become famous through Hu Shi's book *Dai Dongyuan de zhexue* (The philosophy of Dai Zhen). The discovery in this book of a work of philosophy that extolled human nature, that is, the accomplishment of having rediscovered in Dai Zhen not just a practitioner of *kaozheng* philology but a great thinker as well, belongs to Zhang Binglin.

The intellectual worlds of the pre– and post–May Fourth eras were full of Zhang's followers, as a quick glance at the names of such men as Lu Xun (1881–1936), Zhou Zuoren (1885–1966), Qian Xuantong (1887–1939), Huang Kan, Wu Chengshi (1885–1939), Zhu Zonglai (d. 1919), Ma Yucao, and Zhu Xizu (1879–1945) will clearly indicate. Let me mention the undoubtedly correct point made by Ren Fangqiu, that the critique of Confucianism, the most important element of the May Fourth Movement, and the anti-Confucian movement drew their inspiration in part from Zhang Binglin's *zhuzi* studies.[3]

Hu Shi once discussed Zhang Binglin along the following lines. Although the era from the late Qing through the early Republic marked the concluding period of Chinese literature in the classical language, the conclusion was a glorious one thanks to

Zhang's unexpected appearance. Through the previous two millennia of Chinese intellectual history, there were only seven or eight superb books that genuinely deserved to be called "works of literature," Hu continued, and Zhang Binglin's essays in *Guogu lunheng* (Disquisitions on the national heritage) and *Jianlun* (Investigative essays) belong on that list of seven or eight, right next to the *Wenxin diaolong* (The literary mind and the carving of dragons), *Shitong* (Historical generalizations) by Liu Zhiji (661–721), and the *Wenshi tongyi* (General principles of literature and history) by Zhang Xuecheng.[4] The two volumes by Zhang that Hu Shi cited were collections of his essays on philology, literature, *zhuzi* studies, historiography, revolutionary tactics, politics, and the like. Although Hu saw in Zhang the culmination of traditional scholarship, one senses in reading these two books that Zhang was also, as I have tried to indicate with the few examples given above, a man forging a pathway into the next era.

Zhang was not solely a scholar, however; he was a revolutionary as well. Indeed, he was a thoroughly uncompromising revolutionary. As is true of the articles collected in his two books mentioned above, his best-known writings—"Xin fangyan," "Wenshi" (The origins of language), and *Qi wu lun shi* (Explanation of "On seeing things as equal"), which explains Zhuangzi's thought on the basis of Weishi Buddhist philosophy—were all written in the whirlwind of the revolutionary movement. In exalting the righteousness of the revolutionary cause and in contributing to the revolutionary current, even the uprisings inspired by Sun Zhongshan and Huang Xing (1872–1916) could not compare with Zhang Binglin's speeches. At the time, Sun Zhongshan's rebellious activities in Canton and elsewhere and the announcement (in Hawaii and Hong Kong) of the Manifesto of the Xing Zhonghui (Arise China Society) were mere local events either on the periphery or overseas. They lacked the capacity to jolt the spirit of Chinese intellectuals generally. What truly awakened Chinese intellectuals living on Chinese soil to an awareness of national revolution and opposition to the reformers was surely Zhang's involvement in the *Subao* case.

Zhang worked painstakingly as editor of *Minbao*, which was

at the far left of the Chinese journalistic world on the eve of the revolution. When the honors were distributed after the victory of the Revolution of 1911 and the plans to confer on Zhang a second-rank honor were revealed, he raised his objections resolutely, yet not in a simply boastful manner:

[Sun] Zhongshan has only the merit of a propagandist, and he is said to be receiving highest honors. Although I'm just a simple man, my merits as a propagandist certainly far exceed Zhongshan's. Following the era of the Boxer Uprising, there were two courses for propagating the revolution. The weak-kneed have been mixed in with the constitutional monarchists, and extremists have pursued fallacious arguments for freedom and equality. The revolution's return to purity followed the publication of my critique of Kang Youwei. . . . When I was later editor of *Minbao*, we gained international attention and rapidly attracted to the revolutionary cause even Qing officials and established scholars. Have we reached the point of pinning our hopes on some scatterbrained youths and a gang tied up in political and legalistic arguments? . . . I absolutely refuse to accept second-rank honors.[5]

At the age of 33 in 1900, Zhang cut his queue in an act of decided defiance toward the Qing state, and he issued his first public anti-Manchu statement with the publication of *Qiushu* (Book of persecutions) the following year.[6] The *Qiushu* is a collection of intellectual, scholarly essays, written in the form of a *zhuzi* work. These pieces are extremely difficult, a characteristic of Zhang's written style; they are hard to so much as punctuate.

The year after that, 1902, at the age of 35, he took refuge for a second time in Japan, to escape investigation by the authorities. There, in Yokohama, he met Sun Zhongshan for the first time. Zhang's first trip to Japan had followed the failure of the 1898 Reform Movement, when the government was preparing to launch a search for him as an identified criminal. At that time he had gone first to Taiwan, and then in 1899 made his escape to Japan. Apparently, he and Sun had been seated together on some occasion during this period in Japan, but they did not know each other. His second exile lasted only about three months, but during that period he made preparations at the Seiyōken Restaurant in Ueno (Tokyo) for the convening of a "Meeting Commemorating the 242nd Year since the Ruination of China" ("ruination" here carried the sense that China, as the nation of the Han people, had been destroyed along with the Ming dynasty at the hands of the Manchus). The effort to hold this meeting was important in the history of the 1911 Revolution. It never came about, for on the appointed day it was banned by the authorities, but the effort marks the beginning of an anti–Manchu revolutionary organization taking shape among the overseas Chinese students in Japan.

The year 1903 witnessed the *Subao* Incident. In this year Zhang wrote his article "Po Kang Youwei lun geming shu" (Letter attacking Kang Youwei's views on revolution), and an introduction to *Geming jun* (The revolutionary army) by the 19-year-old youth Zou Rong (1885–1905); and the Shanghai newspaper *Subao* quoted from them. *Subao* was then under the editorial hand of Zhang Xingyan (1882–1973), a revolutionary who had sworn an oath of brotherhood with Zhang Binglin, and the paper had close ties with the revolutionary Patriotic Public School, then being run by Cai Yuanpei (1869–1940) and Huang Zongyang. Zhang Binglin was a teacher in this school at the time. In this connection, the fact that Zhang Shizhao, who would later become an enemy of Lu Xun, Xu Guangping (1907–68), and others, was the very same Zhang Xingyan makes the relationship between Lu Xun and Zhang Binglin even more curious.

In his "open letter" to Kang Youwei, Zhang fiercely refuted Kang on fourteen points, arguing that Kang had been answering overseas Chinese in America, carrying out political reforms under the ægis of the present emperor as a route to progress in contemporary China, trying to establish a constitutional form of government, and arguing that revolution would lead China to destruction. This was the first debate posing in opposition the principles of reform and those of revolution, and Zhang omitted nothing in laying out his contrary point of view. On occasion in this debate, Zhang referred to the emperor without the proper honorific titles of address—in fact, he shocked the world by insulting him as "the despicable little ignorant wretch" (literally, someone who cannot tell the difference between a bean and a noodle). On a complaint issued by the Qing government, Zhang was arrested by the Concession Police of the Shanghai Municipal Council and sentenced to three years in prison. Had he been apprehended outside the Foreign Concession area, he surely would have been in danger of losing his life.

After completing each day's compulsory labor in prison, Zhang would concentrate on reading Buddhist sutras. Of course, he had read extensively in the Buddhist canon long before this, but while in prison he read, in particular, works such as *Yinming ruzheng lilun* (The theories of [ancient Indian] Buddhist logic), a text on Buddhist logic, as well as two Weishi Buddhist works, *Cheng Weishi lun* (Treatise on the completion of Weishi), and *Yujia shidi lun* (Yogācāra-bhūmi-śāstra). These ultimately had an enormous impact on his scholarship and thought.

While in prison, Zhang also wrote an extremely influential essay entitled "Guimao yuzhong ziji" (Personal note from prison in 1903). One must read this piece to understand Zhang Binglin as an individual and as a thinker. It reads in part as follows:

Heaven has conferred upon me the national essence (*guocui*). Thirty-six years have elapsed from the time of my birth to the present. "The phoenix does not come; the river gives forth no chart" [implying that no sages have come to save the world; *Lunyu*, "Zihan," section 8]. I cannot bear sitting calmly in my place. I must trace the steps of the "uncrowned king" and the "poor official." However, does this simply mean that I should cherish broken and worn-out things? With our people and our culture in their proper places, I must seek to irradiate their magnificence. My will has not yet achieved its end. I am still shackled by the enemy state. Others will follow me to renew the golden flame. If our nation's antiquity and our people's historical record come to an end in my hands and China's broad and magnificent scholarship should ultimately find its continuance severed, this will be my crime to bear.[7]

"Uncrowned king" refers to Confucius, reputed author of the *Spring and Autumn Annals*; "poor official" refers to Zuo Qiuming, author of the *Zuozhuan* or *Zuo Commentary* (on the *Spring and Autumn Annals*). To "trace the steps" of Zuo Qiuming implies advocacy of the great cause of "nationalism." To "cherish broken and worn-out things" implies simple study of ancient documents without the kind of devotion Zhang felt. The "enemy state" refers to the Qing, and "to renew the golden flame" to the revolutionary movement.

After serving three years in prison, Zhang was released in late June 1906, Zou Rong having died there the previous year. He was greeted by members of the Tongmenghui (Revolutionary Alliance) sent by Sun Zhongshan, who took him directly from the prison gates to the wharf, whence he proceeded to Japan. From this point forward Zhang's activities both as a revolutionary and as a scholar entered the period of his highest achievement. On July 15, 1906, a group of overseas Chinese students in Japan met and threw a welcoming party for Zhang at the Kinkikan in the Kanda section of Toyko. Despite the rain that day, some two thousand people attended. First there were greetings from the sponsors of the meeting, followed by Zhang's own speech, which was in turn followed by speeches by Miyazaki Tōten (1870–1922) and a number of the Chinese students in attendance that day. The meeting finally broke up at midnight. Zhang's speech was carried in the revolutionaries' journal *Minbao* (issue no. 6), and it is translated below.

After the victory of the revolution late in 1911, Zhang took a post as privy counsellor to the Republican government. He also served in Changchun as a frontier defense official for the three eastern provinces, better known as Manchuria. When he later refused to respond positively to the desires of Yuan Shikai (1859–1916) to accede to the imperial throne, he was placed under house arrest in Beijing for nearly three years; for a time, according to his autobiography, all his funds were exhausted and he went without food for seven or eight days. With Yuan's unexpectedly sudden death, Zhang escaped from these dire straits.

In a letter of May 23, 1914, to his wife, Ms. Tang, Zhang explained that he was on the verge of death by starvation and requested that she handle matters for him after his death. He went on: "I did not die on the day I was interrogated by the Qing government, and I shall die after the establishment of a Republic—what further is there to say? After my death, Chinese culture will collapse."[8]

When the Hufa (Protect the Constitution) Army arose the following year (1917), Zhang went to Guangdong to work with Sun Zhongshan as secretary-general of the military regime there. He took part in the fighting in the provinces of Yunnan and Sichuan, traveling some 14,000 li (roughly 5,000 miles), planning strategy for the military. Later he left politics altogether, lived in seclusion in Shanghai, and in his last years established "Mr. Zhang's Institute for National Learning" in Suzhou. There he devoted himself to the study and preservation of China's national learning. However, in the year of the Manchurian Incident (1931), he could no longer suppress his patriotic feelings. He traveled to North China specifically to assist in policy formulation for the defense of that region against the Japanese, and he met with Zhang Xueliang (b. 1898).

In his speeches and essays published after his retirement, one finds much of the "perverse reactionary," and these were indeed used by militarists and reactionary politicians [as his critics have argued]. Nonetheless, this marks no sudden rupture, for he evinced virtually no basic points of conflict with his earlier views as a revolutionary. To preclude the possibility of being misunderstood, I originally referred to him as a "reactionary revolutionary."

Kita Ikki (1883–1937) once called Zhang Binglin "China's Rousseau."[9] However appropriate this comparison may be, we can see that both men appealed to patriotism and emancipation and both profoundly stirred the hearts of others; further, in the essential elements of their ideas, the two men shared a certain deep tie to an anachronistic ideal. For a revolutionary, Zhang probably lived too long. The revolution he espoused was one of "restoration." It was to return Chinese civilization and the people's lives, sullied and enslaved by the Manchu rulers, once again to their original, glorious form. Occasionally, he even called this "revenge." Perhaps Zhang's mission insofar as he was a "revolutionary" ended with the victory of the 1911 Revolution. Yet, in that context his contributions were enormous. It would have been appropriate for Sun Zhongshan's government to have awarded Zhang "highest honors" for his service to the cause.

I have not taken it upon myself to introduce all the facts surrounding Zhang Binglin as a revolutionary or as a scholar. The best source on the former is Onogawa Hidemi's "Shō Heirin no minzoku shisō" (Zhang Binglin's nationalist thought).[10] I leave the latter to the proper person. My aim here is to discuss the place where these two themes cross—namely, to analyze how Zhang Binglin linked national learning or *guoxue* to revolution.

Zhang's Relationship with Lu Xun

The name of Zhang Binglin evokes no response at all among Japanese intellectuals generally, aside from those who do research on Chinese scholarly matters. He is scarcely remembered even as the quaint old man about whom Akutagawa Ryūnosuke (1892–1927) wrote in his travel account of 1921, *Shina yūki* (Record of a voyage to China).[11] Happily, though, as Lu Xun's writings have begun recently to be widely read, Zhang's name will probably gain unforeseen popularity. "Teachers" for whom Lu Xun continued to cherish a deep respect and love throughout his life were extremely few, but Zhang Binglin was one of them, perhaps the only one besides the famous Mr. Fujino Genkurō. Strangely, teacher and disciple both died in 1936, Zhang in June at the age of 69 and Lu in October at the age of 56. Ten days before his death, Lu wrote an article in which he combined reason and sentiment, "Some Recollections of Zhang Taiyan," in memory, as well as in defense, of Zhang. A few days later, Lu supplemented this piece with another, "A Few Matters Connected with Zhang Taiyan." These were probably the last things Lu Xun ever wrote. According to Xu Guangping, these two pieces were left separately, in unpublished draft form, indicating that Lu may have planned to write more about Zhang.[12]

Lu received instruction in *guoxue* or national learning from Zhang during his period of study overseas in Japan (1908, when Lu was 27 years of age); he studied philology and phonology with Zhang. Zhang was then a refugee for the third time, serving as editor of *Minbao*, organ of the Tongmenghui, and engaged in revolutionary activities. He was also lecturing on *guoxue* at the request of the Academy of National Learning, which had been organized principally by overseas Chinese students. It was the latter that Lu Xun attended.[13] The lectures Lu heard were not at the regular Academy but part of the special classes. Zhang was offering special lectures every Sunday morning on the *Shuowen jiezi* (Analysis of characters as an explanation of writing), an ancient Chinese dictionary, at his own home (also headquarters of *Minbao*) in Shinkogawa-chō, Koishikawa, Tokyo, and it was this series of lectures that Lu heard. There were eight young men in the audience, among them: Zhou Zuoren, Lu Xun's younger brother; Xu Shoushang (1882–1948), a lifelong friend of Lu's who was murdered in Taiwan after the end of the war; Qian Xuantang, who would later encourage Lu to write "Diary of a Madman" and later still became Lu's enemy; Zhu Zonglai, who together with Qian later lectured on philology at Beijing University; and Zhu Xizu, who later became a professor at Beijing University.

Lu Xun returned to China less than a year after these lectures, but for the remainder of his life his devotion to Zhang would never waver. What he had learned from Zhang was not merely a specialized knowledge of Chinese philology. As he put it in his essay "Some Recollections of Zhang Taiyan":

To my mind, his contribution to the history of the revolution is actually greater than that to the history of scholarship. I remember over thirty years ago, when his *Qiushu* was first printed, I could neither read nor even punctuate the sentences, let alone understand them; and the same was true of many young people in those days. I heard the name Zhang Taiyan not because of his studies in the Confucian classics and ancient philology, but because he had attacked Kang Youwei, had written a preface to Zou Rong's *The Revolutionary Army*, and was imprisoned in the International Settlement jail in Shanghai. At that time some Chinese students from Zhejiang in Japan were bringing out a magazine called *Tides of Zhejiang*, and it published Zhang's poems written in jail, which were not so difficult to understand. These poems stirred me so much that I still remember them. . . .

In June 1906, immediately following his release from jail, Zhang sailed for Japan and went to Tokyo, where he soon was editing *Minbao*. I liked this paper, not for his old-fashioned and difficult prose style or his treatises on Buddhist philosophy and "bilateral evolution," but for his campaigns against Liang Qichao, who supported retaining the monarchy, against Wu Zhihui and Lan Gongwu, who claimed that to study *Dream of the Red Chamber* was the way to attain Buddhahood. He really put up a gallant and inspiring fight. I also listened to his lectures during this time, not just because he was a good scholar but because he was at the same time a revolutionary, so that today I can still recall his expressions and gestures but not a word of the ancient philology about which he lectured.

Lu Xun concluded this tribute to Zhang as follows:

Those polemical essays are the greatest and most lasting monument to his career. To my mind, even if these pieces are incomplete, they should be collected and published so that he may live in the hearts and minds of those who are now fighting.[14]

"Although Zhang Binglin was a rather excitable character around big shots," wrote Lu Xun's brother Zhou Zuoren, "he was quite mild-mannered with students and could chat lightheartedly with family and friends alike. In the summer, he would sit cross-legged on a mat and slip on his long vest. With his arms bare and growing a tiny, thin mustache, he would joke in a way that rang with seriousness, lecturing with a sly smile on his face. It was at such times that he looked just like the black bodhisattva."[15]

Zhang apparently also loved informal conversations. His favorite among the students for such talks was Qian Xuantong. When people came to partake of such enjoyment with him, Zhang would "crawl on his knees" over to his mat. As a result, Lu Xun awarded him the rather vulgar name *palai paqu* (creeper). The taciturn Lu Xun rarely spoke up. As Xu Shoushang recalled, only once did Lu's views differ from those of Zhang Binglin, and the issue in question concerned the definition of literature.[16]

When it began to become apparent in word and deed that, following the 1911 Revolution, Zhang Binglin was being used in every conceivable way by the forces of reaction, tremendous dissatisfaction arose among his former disciples. This discontent reached its zenith when Zhang, in support of the Guomindang's crushing of the Chinese Communist Party, openly praised Zeng Guofan (1811–72) as a model of human morality. Earlier, Zhang had repudiated Zeng for having resigned himself to being a running dog of the Manchu court and a traitor who had destroyed the Taipings, forerunners of the national revolution. Zeng was later condemned by the revolutionaries, but in the eyes of the Qing dynasty he was an official who served meritoriously in its restoration and was given posthumous honors.[17] As Zhou Zuoren wrote:

"It looks as if my teacher has discarded the righteous cause of [Han] restoration championed for the past forty years. I must believe this; my teacher must not act in such a way; such a person cannot be my teacher." So wrote Zhang Binglin in a piece entitled "Taking Leave of My Teacher," before he parted company with his revered teacher Yu Yue.[18] I could not have foreseen it, but I now have also reached the point of having no choice but to take my leave and part company with my teacher [Zhang Binglin].[19]

Zhou Zuoren's indignation, as expressed in this citation, seemed genuinely warranted. There were indeed countless contradictions and inconsistencies in Zhang's personal writings and activities. Lu Xun, however, remained steadfastly silent and withheld all criticism. In a letter he subsequently wrote, he had the following to say on the subject:

In the past, [Chinese] reverence for teachers knew no bounds. I feel rather antipathetic toward this point. If a teacher errs, I believe opposition to be in order. In cases, however, where a teacher though innocent is met with suggestions of illegality, one cannot save oneself by opportunistically throwing stones and currying favor with one's enemies. Although Professor Zhang once taught me philology, because I later advocated the vernacular in writing I had to visit him on two occasions. Later, when Zhang advocated [an ancient ritual known as] *touhu* [supported at the time by the warlord Sun Chuanfang], I harbored private opposition to this, but when the Guomindang attempted to confiscate Zhang's dilapidated house, I in no way sought to curry favor with the authorities. Should I henceforth meet him, I shall respectfully treat him in a manner befitting a teacher and a disciple. [Zhang also never treated a disciple with arrogance, but always with the peace and harmony befitting friends.] This, I believe, is the way teachers and disciples should act toward one another.[20]

Let me refer once more to Lu's "Some Recollections of Zhang Taiyan" on this point:

After the 1911 Revolution, since his ideal was realized he ought to have accomplished great things, but he remained in obscurity. This was quite unlike Maxim Gorky, who was highly respected during his lifetime and honored after death. I think the reason for the difference in their fates was that all Gorky's dreams came true. He personally identified himself with the masses, sharing their joys and anger, their pleasures and sorrows. But whereas Zhang's will to overthrow the Manchus was realized, his desire "first to give the people faith through religion so as to improve the morality of the nation; and second to arouse their sense of ethnicity [nationalism] through the national essence [*guocui*] so as to improve their patriotism"[21] was merely a visionary ideal. Herein lies the basis of the difference between the two men. So, when Yuan Shikai usurped state power to serve his selfish ends [and become emperor], Zhang further lost any real base, and nothing was left to him save empty writing. He had cut himself off from the people and grew by degrees more and more neglected.[22] Later, he even took part in the revival of the ancient *touhu* ritual and accepted presents from powerful people; for this he is frequently reproached by his critics. But this was no more than a blemish in pure jade, certainly no serious stain on his character as a whole. When we consider his career, what other man of his time dared to dangle his revolutionary medal on his fan and go directly to the president's house to rebuke Yuan Shikai's treachery? What other man of his generation remained firm in his revolutionary will despite seven persecutions and three prison sentences? This was the spirit of a man of wisdom, a model to future generations. Recently, some philistines have written articles for the press that jeer at him haughtily. This should amply prove the sayings: "A low mind thinks the worst of everyone," and "A tiny insect, trying to shake a mighty tree, is ludicrously ignorant of its own weakness."[23]

Critical assessments of Zhang Binglin have varied enormously. Bearing in mind that Zhang denounced Japan and Japanese scholars in every way imaginable, one would not expect to find that he left a good impression on the Japanese scholarly world. There is an element of truth on both sides. While I for one do not believe, for example, that Zhou Zuoren's indignation at the time was "insincere," neither do I think that Lu Xun's defense was completely justified. Nonetheless, I still want to ally myself with the words of Lu Xun as the definitive elegy for Zhang.

I like to think that there was a spiritual, personal, "blood" relationship between Lu and Zhang. In his book *Lu Xun shiji kao* (An examination of Lu Xun's biography), Lin Chen assesses three areas in which Zhang influenced Lu. The first was an indomitable revolutionary spirit; the third was a simplicity and straightforwardness of attitude. Whether these two should ultimately be called influences would seem of secondary importance compared to the deeper question of "blood" relatedness. Zhang once spoke about the idea of "compassion" (*ai*),[24] but in its contemporary, general meaning, "compassion" seems inappropriate to the quality of this "blood" relatedness. I cannot express it well, but Lin's second point hits the mark accurately, I believe, in pointing to the influence on Lu Xun of Zhang Binglin's literary style.

Zhang revered the Wei–Jin period's [classical] style of prose composition in which a simple elegance was the rule. Lu Xun's youthful writings in *guwen* were profoundly learned in the prose style of the Wei–Jin era. Liu Bannong [also known as Liu Fu] once presented Lu Xun with the following couplet: "The theories of Tolstoy and Nietzsche, the prose style of Wei and Jin." All his friends regarded it as perfectly appropriate, and Lu Xun himself did not oppose such a statement. In his introduction to "Fen" (The grave) and elsewhere, he confessed that the prose of his early writings "was written in phrases and with ancient characters I never became fully comfortable with," but this "reflects the influence of Zhang Binglin." When Lu Xun later began to write in the vernacular, he would still on occasion write a piece in the literary style, and it would be in the Wei–Jin style.[25]

Yet, it was not simply a matter of style. Zhang and Lu shared a deep interest in the personages of the Wei–Jin period as well. On reading a piece such as Lu's "Wenhua pianzhi lun" (On the inclinations of culture),[26] I feel certain that at least the young Lu Xun learned a great deal from Zhang Binglin in the intellectual area, too.

Zhang Binglin's Speech in Tokyo, July 15, 1906

I am profoundly grateful for all your kindness today in convening this welcoming meeting for me.[27] My gratitude grows even greater when I look back over my life and see just how worthless it has been. I would like to sum up my career to this point and to assess what should be done today.

When I was young, I read the *Dong hua lu* (Records from within the Eastern Flowery Gate) of Mr. Jiang [Liangqi, 1723–89]. In it I ran across the incident involving Dai Mingshi (1653–1713), Zeng Jing (1679–1736), Cha Siting (1664–1727), and others, and it stirred me to anger. I felt that an alien people had wrought havoc in China, which became a matter of the greatest sadness for us. Later, I read the works of Zheng Suonan [Zheng Sixiao, 1239–1316] and Wang Chuanshan [Wang Fuzhi], and a nationalist way of thinking aimed solely at the protection of the Han people gradually took hold within me. However, there was nothing that might be called a theory in the ideas of these two authors.[28]

Following the Sino-Japanese War of 1894–95, I read through writings from countries East and West, and for the first time I grasped a theory embedded in them. When I advanced the view to my friends at that time that we should drive out the Manchus and plan for our independence, invariably they shook their heads; some thought it was crazy, others said it amounted to rebellion, and some felt it would ensure our being killed. I, however, took advantage of those who branded me a madman and continued to harbor my "mad" thoughts as before.

In the spring of 1902, I came to Japan [for the second time] and there met Sun Zhongshan. There were at that time some overseas students who had come here to work with Sun, but only one or two might have been called Sun's comrades-in-arms—with the others casually coming and going. Sun struck me as a strange man; I became curious and decided to go see him. I found that he was utterly lacking in wholehearted devotion to the idea of saving the Han race. So, the "mad" desires of my private thoughts seemed as unattainable as ever. Instead, I donned the robes of a

Buddhist and became a monk, intent, I believed, on shutting off contact with those in the scholarly and political arenas.

After three years in prison, I have returned here once again, and the number of people who support me has risen a hundredfold. I now realize for the first time here that our thinking has definitely advanced. Earlier, everyone supported the notion of overthrowing the Manchus and reviving the Han people, but it lay dormant within them. Now, for the first time, it has come forth into the light. Until this point I argued, in a word, that "the crane knows when it is midnight, and the rooster knows when it is dawn." Originally, neither midnight nor dawn was a thing that cranes or roosters would have been expected to discern. But, they possessed an innate sense and called out loudly in a single bird voice, and human beings awoke and began to work. There must be a reason for existence. The theory of nationalism that all of you here today espouse is perfectly accurate, and the wild goose has truly taken the lead. I am from an earlier generation and am incapable of achieving anything.

I have another matter I would like to discuss today. Generally, human beings never admit that they themselves are mad. Brilliant poets or great artists who howl in the mountains are different, but everyone else fits this rule. Yet, I alone confess that I am mad, that I suffer from a nervous disorder. What's more, when I hear it said that I am mad or nervous, I become elated.[29] Why is that so?

Ordinarily, it is neurotic people who arrive at "profound thoughts that transcend common knowledge" [often said of the *Spring and Autumn Annals*], and having hit upon such thoughts, they do not attempt to verbalize them. Even if they do speak up, only neurotic people can achieve a deep, unflinching faith when they confront privation and hardship. Thus ever since antiquity, men who amassed great learning and accomplished great deeds were able to do so, in the first instance, because they were neurotic.

Take the case of Socrates. Was he not neurotic? And Rousseau, who advocated popular rights and liberty—did he not jump over a river to chase a dog?[30] He was completely neurotic. And it is an established theory of contemporary scholars of religion that Mohammed, the founder of Islam, was an anal-retentive. The same is true for us of the Han race. The military strategy of Xiong Tingbi (1569–1625) of the Ming period was unparalleled before or since, but it is amply clear that, when you examine the history of his temperament, he was mad. Recently, Zuo Zongtang (1812–85) protected the Manchu wretches and murdered our comrades. As a person he is beneath our consideration, but the tactics he used for victory with unanticipated methods nonetheless deserve our admiration. I think that all sorts of strange things, with which everyone is acquainted, took place at the Yuelu Academy when Zuo Zongtang was a young man. One more example is Bismarck, of Germany. He once had occasion to call a servant, and when there was no answer, he instantly drew his pistol. Indeed, he had a neurotic temperament.

When you consider closely the great deeds of these six men, all were accomplished out of neurosis. Thus, I admit to being a neurotic, and I hope that each of you harbors a bit of neurosis as well. On the basis of what you have just heard, it is useless to worry, in my view, if so and so is neurotic or if someone else is. Yet what can be pondered is the following: when wealth and success are dangled before your eyes as an incentive to cure such neurosis, you can reject the offer. A bit preferable at present would be for people who, although not cured by the nutrients of wealth and success, are cured by the powerful medicine of suffering. In short, one cannot amount to anything once one's steps are no longer taken boldly.

I have taken such strong medicine many times. Let me count how many times: since 1898, I have been wanted by the police seven times; six times I was not apprehended, but the seventh time I was caught. The first three times, I was probably implicated in something, rather than the direct object of an investigation, during a mass roundup of reformist groups. In each of the last four times, the reason was my support for throwing the Manchus out and independence [for China]. In the whirlpools of suffering, however, this is not all that I have endured. No matter what medicine I consume, my neurosis will not be cured. Perhaps it is for this reason that you offer the respect you give me here today. In any event, no matter who it is, if he is neurotic, his work is certain to be a mess and lacking any semblance of order. However, the neurosis about which I speak is not at all the neurosis of someone who is an irresponsible braggart who becomes enraged at the drop of a hat. Coherent, meticulous thought is always clogged up for such a neurotic as this. For example, thought is freight, neurosis the steamship. Empty neurosis, lacking thought, amounts to nothing at all, of course. But without neurosis, can thought make a person move? What I have said thus far amounts to a general outline of my life.

Come what may now, inasmuch as politics, law, strategy, and the like have been thoroughly studied already, there is no need for further talk about them. In my view, human emotions are the most important thing, for without them even a million Napoleons and Washingtons could not bring solidarity to the minds of men. Long ago Plato once said, "The emotions are like inebriation," and this is just like neurosis. In order to perfect the emotions, two things are most important. The first is to arouse religious belief so as to promote national morality; the second is national essence [in the sense of national learning] to stir up the race and build patriotic fervor.

Let me first address the issue of religion. Recently, men such as Bentham and Spencer have offered great praise for profit and shown no concern whatever for religion. Without religion, however, morality can never be advanced. The struggle for existence is solely for the individual. Even if men band together, like dry American flour they cannot harden into noodles. Religion in Europe and the United States reveres Jesus Christ, and it is utter rubbish. Without this Christianity of theirs, however, they absolutely would never have reached the position they have today. In the sociology of [Benjamin] Kidd, there is an attack on the theories of Spencer.

Of our Chinese religions, which one should we choose? With respect to Confucianism [advocated as a religion by Kang Youwei and his reformist supporters], Confucianism was originally something superior. Although in all religions the mysterious and unknowable are blended in, only in the case of Confucianism is this rather more clear-cut. Yet this has its negative points as well. In other words, the era of Confucius himself was one in which aristocrats held political authority, and the commoner class played no role in government. So in planning for the struggle with the aristocrats, Confucius educated 3,000 disciples and trained them to be talented bureaucrats. Commoners subsequently came to play a role in government. Yet, Confucius was a man of little spirit. While planning for the struggle with the aristocracy, he did not try to align himself with the commoners to overthrow the aristocratic political structure. In his *Spring and Autumn Annals*, one finds his theory "denying hereditary officials," but for all his verbal and written abuse, he did not truly embrace this idea. Thus the education of his disciples was that of a husband of his bride; it was, as much as possible, as instructor to the emperor or assistant to the king, and was never aimed at gaining the position of the emperor itself. At the lowest levels, among the warehouse and animal husbandry officials, they were to hang on patiently.

As you all know, Confucius's career rested solely on the king of the state of Lu when he was acting as proxy for the prime minister. Later, Confucius traveled around the 72 states many times before retiring to his hometown late in life. At that time he became dependent on the Ji clan [the imperial Zhou clan]. One can only say that with each passing day, Confucius's spirit dwindled. Thus the greatest stain on Confucianism is that it does not make people rid themselves of the attachment to wealth and success.[31]

Ever since the efforts of Emperor Wu of the Former Han dynasty to honor Confucianism alone, the number of people intent on gaining wealth and success has only increased with time. Today, we are intent on carrying out a revolution and advocating popular rights; hence, we have not the least confusion in our minds about wealth or material success. We are like a bacillus come to infect the entire body. Confucianism can never be adopted.

Furthermore, although Christianity has proved advantageous for Westerners who adopt it, there is no advantage for China in adopting it. In other words, for Chinese to believe in Christianity would mean praying not to God, but to a Western emperor. The elite uses this pretext to study English or French and brags that they are just common men. The next category down, a group poor and without means, borrows this argument to get by from day to day. The lowest group uses the influence of the church to take ignorant villagers to task and to tyrannize their fellows. Thus, Christianity in China is, in every instance, a false Christianity. True Christianity does not exist. If it was a genuine Christianity, we would not be able to embrace it today. True Christianity, if adopted by barbarians, can advance civilization day by day, but when adopted by civilized nations, it has the opposite effect and returns them to barbarity.

For example, politics and scholarship in ancient Rome were glorious indeed, but once Christianity was adopted, philosophy could no longer be studied and all ideas of human liberty were systematically excluded. Scholarship declined, the government fell into disorder, and Rome ultimately perished. The Germanic peoples who subsequently arose were originally lowly, barbarous groups, but once they adopted Christian morality, they gradually cultivated their violent, savage minds, which enabled their civilization to progress. Is this not the most conclusive proof?

Perhaps China today cannot really be compared to Rome, but comparing them is an interesting exercise. Certainly, the Germanic tribes in the early period cannot stand beside Rome. Thus, even if this were genuine Christianity, it would be wholly a negative thing, without advantage, for China. Furthermore, even in the realm of theory, it is bogus and laughably unsubstantial. And the fact that it is inconsistent with philosophy evidently shames those believers with a smattering of learning or thought. This point, too, requires no further elaboration.

Since Confucianism and Christianity are both clearly useless, what religion would be best to adopt? Our country was once hailed as a Buddhist nation. The most sagacious men once had no choice but to place their beliefs in Buddhist theory, while the least intelligent were also compelled to follow Buddhist precepts. It was accepted from top to bottom. The Buddhism that is practiced today, though, has picked up all sorts of impurities, making it different from the original religion. Useful indeed would be discussion of the measures needed for its reform. Take, for instance, the Pure Land sect, most revered by ignorant men and women. What it seeks is merely comfort in the contemporary world and blessings for one's descendants.

In the past, those engrossed in the examination system confused the Pure Land sect with the most idiotic [Daoist] works, such as *Taishang ganying pian* (On Laozi's spiritual empathy) and *Wenchang dijun yinzhi wen* (On the secretly determined [blessing for good works] by the god of literature). Jumbling these together with Pure Land teachings, they burned paper money for idolatrous reasons; they believed in prophecies and oracles; and they received revelations. None of these stupid, disgraceful things are sanctioned by Buddhist scripture, but they were nonetheless haphazardly adopted by the people. Thus, Buddhist believers are now the lowest, most vulgar sort, lacking so much as a smidgen of bravery or fearlessness.

We are now divided into two Buddhist sects, Huayan and Weishi, and we must transform them from what they have been in the past. The gist of what Huayan calls for is "to rescue all living things everywhere," "to refuse to abandon one's head, eyes, and brain on behalf of all living creatures." It is most useful to morality. What Weishi advocates is that all concrete material existence and all formless ideal existence are, in a word, merely subjective illusions, never things that really exist. In recent times, men such as Kant and Schopenhauer have been called philosophical sages throughout the world. Yet, Kant's "twelve categories" are no different from the Weishi Buddhist idea of *xiang fen*; Schopenhauer's view that "the establishment of the world is due solely to the blind actions of the wild" is the same as the theory of "twelve causes and effects" [source unknown]. Many philosophical ideas these men did not discover can still be found here [in Buddhism]. That is why Germans today esteem Buddhism so highly; philosophically, its time has come.

With this belief intact, we can now create a courageous, fearless citadel of our accumulated spirit to draw on for the tasks at hand.

Although one finds in Buddhism numerous theories of salvation through faith, in Huayan and Weishi there is no difference among the three elements of heart, the Buddha, and all living creatures. My reliance on the Buddha, the founder of Buddhism, is in short a reliance on my own heart. Christians rely on their God as one would lean against a wall or against a mountain. Are we not superior by comparison?

Some people ask why Buddhism has been so inefficacious despite the two thousand years it has existed in China. This is an important point. Religions in general can be divided into three sorts: polytheist, monotheist, and atheist. These precisely match three forms of government: aristocracy, monarchy, and republicanism. Of course, one must pass through the monarchy stage before one can enter the republican form of government. If the transformation from aristocracy to republicanism could be made all at once, the republican government would include all sorts of aristocratic impurities.

Daoism in ancient China was polytheistic. Later, Buddhism came to China, but it was atheistic. The intermediate stage was passed over, so people thought that the Buddha was a kind of deity, mixing in the Buddha as one of the many Daoist deities. The result now is the burning of paper money for idolatrous purposes, belief in prophecies and oracles, and the reception of revelations. Such figures as Yuan Liaofan [Yuan Huang, 1533–1606], Peng Shaosheng [Peng Chimu, 1740–96], and Luo Yougao [Luo Taishan, 1734–79, all lay monks of the Ming and Qing eras] all engaged in these practices. All ordinary laymen fell into the same trap as these individuals. Thus, Buddhism proved thoroughly ineffective. Now monotheistic Christianity has arrived in China, and with the power to purify, it has destroyed polytheism. As a result, if Buddhism is put into practice anew, the effects will surely be startling.

Some people ask why the [Chinese] nation has perished if there are Indians who believe in Buddhism. This too raises an important point. That is because, insofar as there is religion in India, there is no government or law beyond it. The laws of Manu are merely the work of Brahmans. In olden times, countries without governments or laws in the end perished regardless of which religion they adopted. In other words, the blame lay not with Buddhism, but with the lack of governments and laws. Since in China we have had government and law, we are most certainly different from India. Lest you disbelieve me in this regard, take a look at Japan. Although a nation of Buddhist believers to be sure, Japan will probably perish in the same way as India has.

Some people say that because Buddhism looks upon all living creatures equally, it can neither give rise to nationalistic thought nor produce a theoretical basis for ousting the Manchus and returning China to the Han people. *Au contraire*: because Buddhism most emphasizes equality, it seeks to expunge that which inhibits equality. Since the Manchu regime treats us Han Chinese in a wide variety of unequal ways, we must naturally drive it out of existence. For example, Buddhism detests the Brahman division of people into four classes. The attitude of the Qing toward us Han Chinese is ten times more hideous than the abuse heaped upon Śudra by Kṣatriya.

Following Buddhist theories, to expel the Manchus and return China to the Han people must become our primary tasks. Furthermore, Buddhism despises monarchical authority. In the precepts of Mahayana Buddhism, it is often stated that "if the king is a tyrant, the bodhisattva has the appropriate authority to depose him." In the classics and commentaries as well, kings and bandits are always lined up alongside one another. Although the Buddha was a prince, he left his family to become a monk. He saw becoming a king as no different from becoming a thief. This view also accords with restoring popular rights. Thus, advocacy of Buddhism is extremely important for social morality, as well as for the morality of our revolutionary army.

Gentlemen, if you all play out your earnest wishes without fear, we can succeed in what our hearts are most devoted to. This will always remain my greatest desire.

I would like next to speak about national essence (*guocui*). Why do I advocate national essence? It is not because I want people to revere Confucianism, but because I want people to cling to the history of our Han people. I speak of history here in its broad sense, which can be divided into three parts: the written language, institutions, and the records of men. Recently, a Westernized Chinese argued that the Chinese people are inferior to Europeans; resigned to despair, China will perish and the yellow race will of necessity be destroyed. This man is unaware of the strengths of China, and without understanding what there is to love about it, his love for the nation and the people becomes shallower with each passing day. Were he to become aware of this fact, even if he lacked the mind of a human being, his love for his nation and his people would become ardent, seething to the boiling point, until it could no longer be curbed.

My saying all this most assuredly has nothing to do with those students of "natural science derived from ancient China" who create farfetched ideas that transform Chinese things into European things.[32] The followers of the Gongyang school claim that the theory of three ages in history is the same as evolutionary theory, and that the nine principles constitute a theory that raises the barbarians' status in China.[33] It is wrong to try to force such views into the shallowest and most inane doctrines of Europe. Let me now summarize the distinctive strengths of our China itself. First, I shall raise the issue of the written language.

The Chinese writing system is completely different from that of all other countries in the world. Each Chinese character has its own original meaning, as well as transformed meanings. In foreign languages when the meanings of words change, there are inflections or declensions reflecting the change, for the same word cannot contain various meanings or connotations. Yet the Chinese language is different. Take, for example, the character *tian*, whose original meaning is "blue sky." Later, its meaning changed, indicating that which is "most revered" and, by further extension, a word indicating "nature." Although these three meanings are not identical, there remains only this one character, *tian*.

Hence one finds in such dictionaries as the *Shuowen jiezi*, the *Erya* (Progress toward correctness), and the *Shiming* (Explanation of names) arguments for *zhuanzhu* [one group of Chinese characters with more than a single reading and concomitant changes in meaning] and *jiajie* [another group of Chinese characters used solely for their sound]. In addition, because Chinese words are different depending on their placement, with the same character capable of being pronounced several different ways, the same thing may have different names. Both the *Erya* and a work known as the *Fangyan* (Dialects) discuss the point that different characters may have the same meaning. In China we call the study of such matters *xiaoxue* or philology, which is a field rather different from what is called "comparative linguistics" in Europe, although they do have certain qualities in common.

One such quality is something philologists of the past did not address. This concerns temporal relations of the era in which a character was created. As a result, there are characters that exist solely in small-seal script (*xiaozhuan*) and not in ancient script (*guwen*) or large-seal script (*dazhuan*); there are characters that exist not in small-seal script, but in square plain script (*lishu*); there are characters that do not exist in the square plain script of the Han dynasty, but can be found in the *Yupian* (Sections of jade) and the *Guangyun* (Expansion of rhymes) dictionaries; and there are characters absent from the *Yupian* and the *Guangyun* but in the *Jiyun* (Collection of rhymes) and the *Leipian* (On classifications). We can surmise a temporal relationship when things came into existence on the basis of the era in which the characters emerged.

In the *Shuowen jiezi*, for example, both *xiong* (now meaning older brother) and *di* (younger brother) are in the *zhuanzhu* category; namely, they both have more than one pronunciation with a comparable number of meanings and are lacking the basic meanings they possess today. This fact would indicate that in the era when ancient men created these characters, they still did not have the expression *xiongdi* (siblings). The character *jun* (ruler) was written in antiquity by a [similar] character read *yin*. Both this character *yin* and that of *fu* (father) were symbols for holding a rod in the hand. Thus, the era in which the ancients created these characters was an era of a wholly familistic political structure.

The distinction between paternal power and ruling power clearly did not exist.

While I cannot discuss each and every case of this sort, the study of this area of learning constitutes a branch of sociology. Without a working knowledge of philology, historical texts cannot be understood at all. Recently, scholars have argued that, because so many new things are appearing from one day to the next, we must hurry up and create new characters to attach to them. While this may certainly be necessary, without a basic knowledge of philology the new characters created may not accord with the rules of the six categories into which all characters fall. In the category in which two characters are combined to create a single word, a shallow understanding of philology will surely lead to inappropriate choices.

In addition, the basis of composition is in fact the written Chinese character. In the Tang dynasty and earlier, literary authors were thoroughly familiar with philology, and as a result their compositions had the power to beautifully move men's emotions. From the Song on, philology gradually waned, and words and technical terms were all used in a random, confused manner, totally lacking the power to move men. In a word, the people of a nation acquire a sense of enjoyment only after they read the compositions of their nation. Which is best: Greek poetry, the poetry of the Rig Veda, or the writings of our own Qu Yuan [343–277 B.C.E.?] and Du Fu [712–70]? For us, of course, the writings of our own ethnic group are superior. Unfortunately, as philology is declining with each passing day, our ability to compose is getting all the weaker. If we support philology and succeed in reviving literature, the power to love our country and protect our people may, before we know it, become magnificent.

The second issue I want to raise is that of institutions. The government of China has generally been one of monarchic autocracy, which has nothing about it worthy of admiration at all. But why did this bureaucratic system have to take the form it did? Why did the political divisions of prefectures and the like have to be made along the lines they were? Why were armies organized as they were? Why did taxes have to be levied as they have been?

There are proper answers to each of these questions, and it will do no good simply to say that autocracies behave in certain ways and ignore the whole problem.

We can only effectively begin to map out concrete plans for the future construction of government when we have asked which elements require reform and which elements need to be revived. What China has been particularly superb at, something the countries of the West can absolutely not approach, is the equitable-field (*juntian*) system; this institution conforms to socialism, to say nothing of the well-field (*jingtian*) system of the Three Dynasties of high antiquity. From the Wei and Jin eras through the Tang, the equitable-field system was in effect. As a result there were no great differences in wealth, and local government was smoothly administered. Consider, if you will, government through the Tang. The government from the Song through the present day can in no way measure up to it. When all is said and done, it was the greatest, the most glorious. All other Chinese institutions are close to socialism. Even if they may have seemed odious, they are still close to socialism.

I would like to raise just two points in this context. One concerns law. Although Chinese law borders on being cruel, from the time that the criminal code was established in the Later Han until today, there has been no expiation of a crime through monetary payment. Only in cases in which women holding official posts would occasionally commit minor offenses, for which the punishment was flogging with the light or heavy bamboo rod, could atonement be purchased. Aside from people of this sort, even if the criminal was wealthy, as in the cases of Tao Zhu and Yi Dun [men of alleged great wealth in the Spring and Autumn period], they had to submit to punishment, just like poor people.

The other point I would like to raise concerns the examination system. The examination system began as a rather inferior institution. Why was it, then, that from the Sui and Tang eras forward, men utilized only the examination system and not the schools? From the Sui and Tang on, books gradually became numerous, and it [becoming educated] was no longer a simple matter as it had been in the Han period. If one entered a school, a large amount of money was needed to purchase books, and the school-work was considerable. Thus, after a time, manual labor and farm work had to be abandoned. Men in the Han era could not plow through the classics with one hand. Since [the examination system, however,] was only poetry and examination essays, for one or two taels of silver, an entire set of model writings could be purchased. By rote memorization of random lines performed as by an actor in a play, manual or farm work could coexist [with one's studies] without being any hindrance at all. Because of such a system, even poor people had hopes of becoming officials. Had this not been the case, study to gain official positions would have to have been left exclusively to the rich. The poor would have sunk to the bottom of the sea, and the day when they participated in political power would not come for a long time.

Although these two points were initially unsatisfactory, they nonetheless contain elements of socialism. This is even truer for something initially good. Our present reverence for Chinese institutions is nothing less than a reverence for our own socialism. What is unsatisfactory must be reformed; what is satisfactory needs to be trusted and followed. These are necessary steps from an emotional standpoint as well.

The third topic I would like to raise is the records of men. Needless to say, there have been merits and demerits among the accomplishments of Chinese personages. However, only a large, excellent, strong, and firm spirit can be subordinate to this for us Chinese. There is no reason for us to study and emulate the stages undergone by Europeans and Americans; we have only to study the steps undertaken by our own Chinese predecessors to regain our original dignity. Among them all, there are two persons who deserve our greatest admiration: Liu Yu [Emperor Wu of the Liu-Song, r. 420–22], who followed the Eastern Jin; and Yueh Fei [1103–41], who attacked the Jin dynasty of the Jurchens during the Southern Song era. Both men led troops in the South and defeated barbarians; they are great boosters of morale.

In the area of scholarship, there are a great many people. Although science did not develop in China, we never fell behind others in the field of philosophy. The philosophies of the Cheng brothers [namely, Cheng Yi (1033–1107) and Cheng Hao (1032–85)], Zhu Xi, Lu Xiangshan, and Wang Yangming [altogether forming the Zhu Xi and Wang Yangming schools] were not all that important. The most learned [of our philosophers] were the "Hundred Schools" or noncanonical thinkers (*zhuzi*) of the Zhou and Qin eras. It is difficult to say off the cuff which of them are good and which bad even in comparison to European and Indian philosophies. Ogyū Sorai [1666–1728] and Dazai Shundai [1680–1747] of Japan cannot possibly be compared to them. Although the Japanese have carried out their Restoration, they endlessly praise the likes of Ogyū Sorai and Dazai Shundai. How is it that we overlook the thought of Zhuangzi and Xunzi?

There is another person of a more recent era. That would be Dai Zhen (also known as Dai Dongyuan), a native of Xiuning county, Anhui province. Dai was a devoted Confucian, but he opposed the Song school or school of principle (*lixue*), and he would always say: "When the law kills someone, sympathy can still be expressed, but when *lixue* kills someone, no such recourse exists."[34] Dai Zhen was born late in the Yongzheng reign of the Manchu dynasty. The Yongzheng Emperor, without any recourse to a legal text at all, censured subjects with his vermillion edicts, and he always said: "Where is your conscience? Aren't you ashamed when you look into yourself and your mind?" These phrases of the Song school were enough for someone to be killed arbitrarily. Men of that time noted that Yongzheng's treatment of people was brutal indeed, but they did not realize that it was in fact *lixue* that fostered this brutality. Suffering under these circumstances, Dai Zhen wrote a thin volume [*Mengzi ziyi shuzheng*, or Evidential analysis of the meanings of terms in the *Mencius*]. At no point in this book did Dai openly attack the Manchus, but anyone who reads it cannot help but despise them. I have noted this point is particular because it might not be at all clear to you.

As I have stated, if you want to build your patriotic fervor, then the most important thing to do is to select someone from all those people of meritorious service or scholarship and never let that person out of your mind. If you cannot find an appropriate person, then ancient events or deeds will suffice to stir everyone's patriotic emotions. In the past Gu Tinglin [Gu Yanwu] contemplated the expulsion of the Manchus, but he lacked military power. So he traveled all around China, investigating ancient inscriptions and the like, and left them to posterity. This is what I have in mind.

Today, I have argued that the two means of dealing with the tasks at hand are unquestionably religion and national essence. My capacity for effort does not go beyond these two items, and I merely ask that what you hope for will be these same two. In short, I want to infect you all with my neurosis, and from there we can infect 400,000,000 people. You are all more than sufficient for the attainment of the principle of nationalism. I intend to take the trouble of proclaiming points of view and publishing journals on your behalf.

National Essence and Revolution

Zhang Binglin deeply admired the scholarship and personal character of Gu Yanwu (born Gu Jiang), the great "nationalistic" scholar of the late Ming and early Qing era and a progenitor of textual criticism or *kaozhengxue*. Zhang adopted the given name Jiang as well, and changed his *hao* to Taiyan [following "*Yanwu*"]. He was born in 1869 in Yuhang county (not Yuyao, where Huang Zongxi and Wang Yangming before him were born), Zhejiang province. His family had been one of scholars for generations and apparently had once been rich. It was, in short, a family of considerable local repute. Zhang's father had worked as a private secretary, as adviser on administrative matters, to the Hangzhou prefectural magistrate. He had passed the examinations and was awaiting appointment as a county magistrate, but he had not been formally appointed. Zhang had two older brothers, both of whom later attained the *juren* degree after passing the second level of the civil service examinations. His eldest brother was the subdirector of studies at the Jiaxing County School, a position equivalent to that of associate professor at a local university. At one point, Zhang's father had had an excellent private collection of books as well. At the time of Binglin's birth, though, this collection was all but gone, and Zhang's father often encouraged his sons to study by referring to the list of books from his old library.

At age 9 Zhang studied the classics with his maternal grandfather, Zhu Youquan (also known as Zhu Youqian). Zhu was patriarch of the clan from which Zhu Xizu, the aforementioned Beijing University professor, hailed. Apparently, Zhu Youquan was a man who entertained a good deal of skepticism for scholars of the day. An ethnic or racial awareness had lain concealed within the Han Chinese consciousness ever since the beginning of the Qing (Manchu) dynasty. For example, it was said that the descendants of Liu Ji (1311–75), a meritorious official of the early Ming dynasty, "were fruitful and reached nearly 10,000 in number," but following the collapse of the Ming, not one of them served as an official for the nearly 300 years of Qing rule. In addition, Chinese scholars had observed that ever since the Taipings had claimed that the Manchus were barbarians and that the Qing court ruled China illegitimately, the Qing court declined continually in national esteem in contrast to the might of the Europeans. As early as thirty years before the 1911 Revolution, there was a rather broad feeling of suspicion among such scholars toward the Manchu regime. Zhejiang province in particular was a culturally advanced area, a kind of humanistic gathering point since antiquity; after the collapse of the Ming, it provided the base for the most stubborn resistance to the Manchus.

Zhang's grandfather told him stories from the period of the Ming-Qing transition and recounted to him the essential points from the writings of such nationalist scholars as Wang Fuzhi and Gu Yanwu. We have spoken of Gu Yanwu, but Wang Fuzhi (Wang Chuanshan) was a major scholar from Hunan province who is generally considered one of the "three great scholars of the late Ming and early Qing" [together with Gu and Huang Zongxi]. This accolade, though, at most dates back to the early twentieth century, for his name and his writings were for a long time unknown. His work was that of a stridently nationalistic philosopher absolutely opposed to any compromise with the

Manchus. The man with sufficient influence to reintroduce Wang's writings was, ironically, Zeng Guofan. Apparently Zeng's aim in publishing Wang's work was simply to bring glory to a former great scholar who came from the same part of China. However, there was a theory current at the time of the 1911 Revolution's high tide that this was Zeng's way of atoning for the sin of contributing to the destruction of the Taipings. Republication of Wang's work occurred four or five years before Zhang was born, which is to say thirteen or fourteen years before the story we are now telling, and locally educated people had already read Wang's work. As Zhang later recalled:

Around the time I was 11 or 12 years of age, Mr. Zhu was teaching me the classics. On one occasion, by chance, the incident involving Zeng Jing that appears in the *Dong hua lu* came up, and Mr. Zhu said: "The sharp distinction between the barbarians and the Chinese carries the same weight as the distinction between master and servant." When I asked if earlier men had discussed this principle, Mr. Zhu responded: "Wang Chuanshan and Gu Tinglin [Yanwu] had spoken of it. Wang in particular stressed it. He pointed out that, although the collapse of dynasties had not differed to any great extent throughout [Chinese] history, the destruction of the Southern Song [by the Mongols] alone spelled the destruction of our tradition and civilization." I asked if the conquest of the Ming by the roving bandit Li Zicheng [i.e., a Han Chinese] was preferable to conquest by the Qing [i.e., Manchus]. Mr. Zhu responded: "This is something best not inquired into at this point. For if Li Zicheng had seized the realm from the Ming dynasty, he still would have been a truly harsh brigand. However, that does not necessarily mean that his descendants would all have been just as cruel. But it's best for you not to ask such questions now." My revolutionary ideas derive from this conversation. As you can see from Mr. Zhu's words, the ideas for a racial revolution are basic to the Han Chinese mind. They have just not come to the surface.[35]

The emotions we have seen in Mr. Zhu were shared by Zhang's father. In a brief biography of his father, Zhang had the following to say:

When I was young, I read a number of discourses by my predecessors and resolved to revive the great works of the Han people through scholarship. My father never dissuaded me from this endeavor. One time he calmly said to me: "Our family has lived for seven or eight generations in the Qing dynasty, and, when we die, we are always placed in the coffin dressed in simple clothing [namely, not garments prescribed by ritual for scholar-officials]. I surely could have obtained a bureaucratic post, but I have never formally held such a position. For when I shall die, I do not want to turn my back on our family precepts. Thus I shall never wear the ritual garb of the Manchu dynasty." I was deeply stirred when I heard this. Since I have devoted myself to our revolution, I have been thrown in prison, and I have been the target of assassins, but I will never be discouraged. Having the good fortune to see my original purpose through to completion will reflect the influence of a heritage passed down through the generations of my ancestors.[36]

There was an expression said to have been popularly transmitted for the nearly three centuries of Manchu rule in China: "In life I submit, but in death I do not; men submit but women do not; the old submit but the young do not." Perhaps Zhang's father fit this mold. Clothing, hairstyles, and the like were by no means trivial matters in China. Traditional Chinese thought holds that each dynasty had its own sumptuary regulations. From the time the Qing began to rule China, the slogan "If you want to keep your head, do not keep your hair; if you keep your hair, you will not keep your head" [that is, shave your hair into a queue] was strictly impressed upon the populace, and bloody incidents involving hair were frequent. When Zhang Binglin later boldly cut off his queue, for the time this could truly be said to be the action of a "maniac."[37]

At age 23 Zhang entered the Gujing Jingshe in Hangzhou, provincial capital of Zhejiang. The Gujing Jingshe was a school, or rather an institute, established by the great textual scholar of the mid-Qing years Ruan Yuan (1764–1849). The head of the institute was then Yu Yue (Yu Quyuan), well-known as a textual scholar of the late Qing. Zhang then began to study orthodox *kaozhengxue* there. His chronological autobiography, though, tells us that at age 18 he first read the *Yishu* (Commentaries) on the Nine Classics of the Tang dynasty; that his older brother taught him methods of classical scholarship; that he read the

Yinxue wushu (Five texts on phonology) by Gu Yanwu, the *Jingyi shuwen* (Writings on the meaning of the classics) by Wang Yinzhi (1766–1834), and the *Erya yishu* (Commentary on the *Erya*) by Hao Yixing; and that he had learned much from all of these scholars. He then proceeded to concentrate on classical scholarship and tried to pattern his prose style after the ancients. The next year [at age 19], he obtained the *Huang Qing jingjie* (Qing exegeses of the classics, a massive compendium edited by Ruan Yuan, which brought together the theories on classical learning of Qing scholars specializing in textual criticism, in 1400 *juan*), and over a two-year period he read it avidly. From this personal account, it is clear that Zhang's preparation for the Gujing Jingshe was more than adequate.

Zhang spent seven full years at the Gujing Jingshe, and this experience established a basis for him as a scholar. He devoted the bulk of his attention to the pure *kaozheng* style of classical research.[38] Thus one can easily imagine how deeply immersed in philology he must have been. Zhang's interests, however, ran beyond this. When he was 21, before entering the Gujing Jingshe, he said, "On the side I pored over the writings of the *zhuzi* as well as works of history, and for the first time I harbored the desire to write." This note would indicate that he was trying to establish his own point of view as a thinker and not just do philological exegeses of classical texts.

Soon after entering the institute, he purchased a copy of the *Tongdian* (Comprehensive encyclopedia) and read it; he would reread it seven or eight times in later years. The *Tongdian* was an institutional history of China by the Tang author Du You (735–812), which not even our Naitō Konan (1866–1934) had read, replete with the author's distinctive point of view. It had little in common with *kaozhengxue*. He read the *Tongdian* with alacrity; and, as he later noted in his chronological autobiography in an entry for age 30, "I took the *Tongdian*, the *Wenxian tongkao* [Comprehensive analysis of writings on culture and institutions, by Ma Duanlin, ca. 1250–1325], and the *Zizhi tongjian* [Complete mirror for aid in government, by Sima Guang, 1019–86] as the basis [of scholarship]." These facts would indicate an attitude somewhat at variance from orthodox *kaozhengxue*.

For example, he denounced Zheng Xuan (127–200), the idol of *kaozheng* scholars. Of Li Zhaoluo (1769–1841), who had clearly turned against philological study, he made special mention: Li "alone mastered the learning of the *Zizhi tongjian*, the *Tongdian*, and the *Wenxian tongkao*."[39] Of Hang Shijun (1696–1773), a true eccentric in the world of scholarship, Zhang wrote: "He assigned to his students the four *tong*: *Tongdian*, *Wenxian tongkao*, *Tongzhi* [Comprehensive record, by Zheng Qiao, 1102–60], and *Zizhi tongjian*."[40] The sense is roughly the same here. In other words, we must recognize the early emergence in Zhang of a deep historical interest in politics and ritual systems, one of his genuine scholarly strengths, as well as his interest in a "national learning" that transcended *kaozhengxue*, which roughly paralleled his interest in philology.

Nor was Zhang anything but concerned with contemporary ideas and politics. In 1896, when Zhang was 28, the Sino-Japanese War was concluded with the signing of the Treaty of Shimonoseki, an inordinately humiliating experience for China. Outraged, Kang Youwei and others tried to save their country by unleashing a spirit of enlightenment and progressiveness and fanning the flames of political reform. They founded the Qiangxuehui (Society for the Encouragement of Learning) and appealed to like-minded souls. Zhang joined early on and sent in his membership fee of sixteen *yuan*. When the Qiangxuehui was suppressed, Kang Youwei's disciple Liang Qichao began publishing a newspaper, *Shiwubao*, in Shanghai, and he invited Zhang to join the editorial staff, where he had an opportunity to meet the young Kojō Teikichi.[41] Unable to mollify Yu Yue's dismay at his taking this step, Zhang accepted Liang's offer and left the Gujing Jingshe.

This was Zhang's first step into an actual political movement—at 28 years of age. Although he wrote nothing about these events, the conclusion of the Sino-Japanese War proved to be an enormous shock to China's intellectuals. However devotedly he was studying *kaozhengxue* at the Gujing Jingshe, Zhang was undoubtedly no exception. In any case, this was the same Zhang who would later vilify the reformism of the Kang-Liang clique in pretty brutal terms, but for a time his name was linked to the editorial staff of this clique's organ, a fascinating event in the history of the Chinese Revolution.

Neither the manifesto of Sun Zhongshan's Xing Zhonghui nor its Huizhou (Waichow) Uprising had by any means electrified the world. Zhang probably knew nothing of these events of earlier years, and during his time with *Shiwubao* he learned for the first time of Sun's existence from the foreign press. At that time intellectuals did not yet generally distinguish between reform and revolution, being altogether focused on one point, the need for "change." If we can leave Kang Youwei aside for the moment,[42] Liang Qichao's writings in support of "change" (*bian*) might be considered revolutionary theories; and Tan Sitong's *Renxue* called for patently revolutionary ideas. By contrast, the two articles Zhang Binglin published for *Shiwubao* were purely reformist in nature.

The first piece (February 1897) was entitled "It Is Best for Asia to Stand Interdependently." It called upon China to link arms with Japan to resist the coercion of the Russians: "It is no exaggeration to say that the spirit calling for a revived Asia will begin with Japan. China will rely on Japan, and Japan will rely on China. If [Japan] observes China's strengths and forges bonds of interdependence, we can hold off the distant West and defend against a closer Russia. The waves on the Pacific Ocean will be calm." Furthermore, he claimed that Japanese and Chinese were of "the same kind" (meaning the same race), and the unfortunate Sino-Japanese War, he argued, was clearly a necessary act of "self-rescue" on behalf of the Japanese vis-à-vis Russia. These points are virtually unbelievable when one looks at the regular jabs Zhang would take at Japan in every conceivable way in later years.

The second essay (March 1897) was entitled "Let Us Immediately Emphasize Great Advantages to the Yellow Race of Certain Schools of Thought." This piece began by advocating a position based on two quotations from the *Gongyang Commentary* on the *Spring and Autumn Annals*, "great unity" and "linking of the three ages." In it, he wrote: "Should we seek to reorganize the schools, we must model them on the points laid down by Huang Zongxi in his *Mingyi daifang lu* (A plan for the prince)." At the end, he noted that the revolutionary trend had become an international spirit as if drawn by force of attraction—it could not be suppressed. However, the destruction caused by discord at the time of revolution would have unhappy consequences for the Chinese people. Foreign enemies would take advantage of incessant civil disturbances and invite a situation like the one that resulted when "the present dynasty established imperial authority" by taking advantage of the chaos brought on by Zhang Xianzhong (1605–47) and Li Zicheng (1605?–45). He concluded that the urgent tasks of the day were to protect the people with proper doctrine and protect the nation with the people; in short, "to forestall revolution with reform."

Years later, Zhang would ridicule these theories from the *Gongyang Commentary* as utterly absurd, and he would attack Huang Zongxi as infamous, indeed as traitorous to the Chinese people. For those who know his denunciation of the Manchu emperor as "a despicable wretch who cannot tell the difference between a bean and a noodle," his language from this early period will strike them as strange. Surely, Zhang's statement in his autobiography that his ideas of an ethnic revolution came to him when he was a youngster is dubious at best. Indeed, there is probably a contradiction here.

Upon enumerating all the lawless, immoral deeds of the Manchus, Tan Sitong once said, "I pray that you Chinese will not think of them, even in your dreams, as compatriots." He also invoked the names of "those men of spirit and virtue [rebels of antiquity, such as] Chen She (Chen Sheng, d. 208 B.C.E.) and Yang Xuangan (d. 613), who laid the groundwork for sages to follow."[43] Yet, Tan served the Qing court as an official and was a leading player in the 1898 Reform Movement. We see a similar problem here in categorizing the reformers. Those who know of Tan Sitong's glorious last moments would certainly never call such actions opportunistic. Nevertheless, a wide array of theories concerning Tan's true intentions spread among the revolutionaries. They all seem to me to go too far. In a word, the period we are discussing predates the strict division that later developed between revolutionaries and reformers. An inchoate impulse to a kind of "radical reform" was aboil. Zhang would later say: "I did once advocate reformism. . . . However, the language is different from its usage today, though the meaning remains the same. In the past, I called for an indirect revolution; now, I call for a direct revolution."[44] This is a half-quibbling, half-accurate record on Zhang's part.

To understand Zhang's spiritual inclinations in his *Shiwubao* period, we cite an entry from his chronological autobiography that may help clarify the events just described.

In the spring of the 23rd year of the Guangxu reign [1897], I was in Shanghai. Liang Qichao and his group were calling for a "Confucian religion," to which I was greatly opposed. . . . At this time, Song Shu [1862–1910, Xu Shouchang's teacher], also known as Song Pingzi, came to Shanghai and we had a talk full of mutual sympathy. Song showed me a copy [undoubtedly in manuscript] of Tan Sitong's *Renxue*. Tan had indiscriminately gathered together any- and everybody's ideas. I couldn't understand it, nor was I the least bit interested. Song asked: "Have you read the Buddhist classics?" I responded: "At the prompting of Xia Zengyou (1865–1924), I have cursorily glanced through such sutras as the Fahua, Huayan, and Nirvana sutras, but without any depth of understanding." Song said: "You should try and read the *Sanlun*" [The Three Treatises: namely, the *Zhonglun* or Treatise on the Middle, the *Bailun* or Treatise on the Hundred Verses, and the *Shiermenlun* or Treatise on the Twelve Gates]. So, I tried to read through them but found I didn't like them at all. It was at this time that I had become enamored of Xunzi's notion of *rushu* [emphasis on ritual and politics and on classical philological research], so I found the expedient of an abstract theory highly displeasing. I would occasionally read the *Dacheng qixin lun* (Treatise on the rise of faith in the Greater Vehicle) for spiritual nourishment, but I didn't enjoy it.

Around this time, new [i.e., Western] learning was very popular in China, and it was all the rage in arguing about politics to throw mathematics and physics into the mix. Liang Qichao was not originally of this sort, and I quite liked the terminology he borrowed for political analysis. Thus, I have always been opposed to the notion that technique and politics are qualitatively different from *shu*; for the latter, I argue, is nothing more than a new model of learning solely for the civil service examinations. Yet, even though the arguments of Song Shu and Chen Fuchen [styled Jieshi, who was Ma Xulun's teacher] were rather solid, I suggested the "School of Yongjia,"[45] and they could not avoid the extraordinary ease of seeing things this way. I based my point of view on the *Tongdian*, the *Wenxian tongkao*, and the *Zizhi tongjian*, with guidance from *Xunzi* and *Hanfeizi*.

Furthermore, whereas Kang's group referred to Huang Zongxi's *Mingyi daifang lu*, I always rebutted them with citations from Wang Fuzhi's *Huangshu* (The yellow book). My point was that if the Manchu regime was not thrown out, all varieties of reform would be merely empty verbiage, and their isms would eventually break up and disperse. However, even in Kang's group one could find people who shared certain revolutionary principles. It would take another four years for this opposition to become perfectly clear.

One sort of person from the revolutionary period, typified by Song Shu (also known as Song Heng), who appears in Zhang's reference above, and by Su Manshu (1884–1918), is extremely interesting, but I cannot touch on them here. Perhaps Zhang's antipathy toward a Confucian religion was a view already current at the time. Despite his evaluation of Tan Sitong's *Renxue*, he remained exceedingly reverential toward Tan himself.[46] However, Zhang's understanding of Buddhism closely resembled that to be found in Liang's biography of Tan Sitong. Perhaps it was only natural that Zhang would strictly adhere to the school of thought or the principles distinctive to *kaozhengxue*, which he had inherited from his forebears. When he eventually indicated his total opposition to the Gongyang school, he only pointed to Liao Ping (1852–1932) and his theories as the oddest elements within the Gongyang clique. Still, this recognition was based on the point that Liao Ping's differentiation between the New and Old Text schools was a sharp distinction.[47]

What about the contrast between Zhang's use of the *Huangshu* and the reformist, Gongyang use of such works as the *Mingyi daifang lu*?[48] Perhaps such a contrast was not recognized, for in his first revolutionary testament, the *Qiushu*, published five years later, in 1901, Zhang expressed extraordinary reverence for Huang Zongxi, saying that he was "indeed a sage."[49] Yet it is easy to see that the diverging of Kang Youwei, Liang Qichao, and others of their persuasion from Zhang was grounded in a fundamental difference of scholarly position.

At the Gujing Jingshe, Zhang had particularly devoted his energies in classical study to the *Zuozhuan*. Whereas the *Gongyang Commentary* was the central classical work of the New Text school, the *Zuozhuan* served, as we have already noted, the same function for the Old Text school. As Zhang himself pointed out: "When I first began my study of the classics, I set out only to learn the ritual systems through philological research. Under Professor Yu's tutelage, my capacities for detailed investigations improved and deepened. However, I did not truly come to an understanding of basic principles. When I was 24 [by Chinese reckoning], for the first time the distinction between the New and Old Text doctrines became clear to me." Although Zhang kept his distance from another teacher at the Gujing Jingshe, Tan Xian (1832–1901, author of the *Futang riji*, Diary of [Tan] Futang, among other works), an admirer of the New Text school, several years later when he met Xia Zengyou, he took no heed of the fact that Xia was an ardent Gongyang advocate, just considering Xia's views wild eccentricities.

Concerning Liu Xin (53? B.C.E.–23 C.E.; also known as Liu Zijun), whom the Gongyang school despised, Kang Youwei had already written his *Xinxue weijing kao* (A study of the forged classics of the Xin period). Kang argued that all the classics in the Old Script were Liu Xin's forgeries and hence not true classics; the genuine classics were those in the New Script. In those New Script classics was to be found Confucius's advocacy of theories and programs for political reform. This question had become a major scholarly issue, and Zhang became sufficiently enamored of Liu Xin to carve a chop for personal use carrying the expression: "Liu Zijun sishu dizi" (privately cultivated disciple of Liu Zijun [Xin]). "Later, I gathered together the view of Xunzi, Jia Yi (201?–169? B.C.E.), Sima Qian (145?–86? B.C.E.), Liu Xiang

(77–6 B.C.E.), and others on the *Zuozhuan*, and, when I was 29, I penned a work entitled *Zuozhuan du* (Reading the *Zuozhuan*)."[50] From these experiences, one would think that Zhang's citations of Gongyang theories in his essays for *Shiwubao* were simply a temporary faltering along the way. In fact, though, the Gongyang school was the new tide of thought in its day, and pure classicists for their part became enormously popular among intellectuals who were critical to a greater or lesser extent of China's contemporary situation. Indeed, even such an old Confucian as Zhang's teacher, Yu Yue, offered his views on issues.[51]

Kang Youwei, Liang Qichao, and their group pursued a clear reformist policy, with the principal aim of establishing a constitutional monarchy in China as a way of moving beyond the status quo. Although they did in fact call for a kind of republic in which a figurehead emperor played a minimal role, ultimately their goal was democracy on the English model, in which the monarch remained. In opposition, Zhang had long been leaning toward radical ethnic revolutionary principles. We must, however, keep in mind the backdrop for this clash of opinions in the different schools of Chinese scholarship.

Originally, the "realm" (or *tianxia*, all under heaven, in Chinese) was formed by Chinese and alien peoples (often referred to as "barbarians") living along China's borders. In the words of the *Zuozhuan*: "The barbarians are jackals and wolves, they must not be accommodated"; and "If they be not of our race, then their hearts must be different." The essential points here were the sharp differentiation between "barbarians" and Chinese and the need to protect China against the "barbarians."[52] Kang Youwei, for his part, built on the work of earlier Qing advocates of the Gongyang position, who had supported the views of such ancient commentators as Dong Zhongshu (179–104? B.C.E.) and He Xiu (129–82). The gist of the *Gongyang Commentary*, in their view, was that the ultimate in societal advancement—"the great unity"—would come about when the distinction between Chinese and "barbarians" disappeared and a fully human society emerged.

In the historical scheme put forward by the Gongyang school

(from disorder to ascending peace to great peace), there was posited an epoch between the first era of disorder (or chaos)—when, again according to the *Gongyang Commentary*, "those states [such as Confucius's state of Lu] lay within and the various Xia [other states inhabited by the Han people] lay without"—and the final era of great peace and unity, when "the barbarians would advance and attain positions of nobility," as the emperor would bestow noble ranks upon them, and they would be treated in the same manner as states comprising Han Chinese. This intervening period of ascending or small peace, in which "the various states of the Xia lay within and the barbarians lay without," was posited as part of the "three ages" theory of the Gongyang school. Accordingly, one finds xenophobia well represented in the Gongyang school as well. Furthermore, anti-foreign thought in the form of anti-Manchuism was more or less the voice of the age itself [as opposed to that of a specific school of thought]. In these early years, as noted above, we cannot necessarily point to anti-foreignism as the defining difference between Zhang Binglin on the one hand, and Kang Youwei and Liang Qichao on the other.

Nonetheless, from the perspective of the opposition between the Gongyang and Zuozhuan schools, this distinction was ultimately to become the decisive criterion separating the reformism of the Kang-Liang group and the revolutionary views of Zhang Binglin. In other words, in the view of the New Text school the Chinese-"barbarian" distinction was reduced to a difference in cultural levels; once the "barbarians" had advanced, any reason for discrimination would disappear. Thus even if one supported an ethnic revolution, it was merely, in their view, a process within the evolution of history. By contrast, in the principles of the *Zuozhuan*, argued Zhang Binglin, the Han-"barbarian" distinction represented the most basic difference in blood—a distinction between "men and wild beasts." For Zhang Binglin, revolution itself was the main objective.

I have already had frequent occasion to point to the disagreement between the various schools over interpretations of the *Spring and Autumn Annals*, so I shall not rehearse it again now.[53] Here, I would like to add a note of opposition to the view that seems so easily to stir the sympathies of Japanese scholars—namely, that on the whole the views of Kang Youwei and Liang Qichao were extraordinarily "scientific" (the two having at the time denounced the ideas of Zhang Binglin and his group on an ethnic revolution as "lacking scientific theory"), and that the attitude of the reformers toward the controversy was unimpeachable. For, they argue, Zhang advocated a racial revolution, something indeed to be despised as base irrationalism. I should like to come to Zhang's defense at this point and add the following note. The "barbarians" referred to in Zhang's concept of nationalism were exclusively the Manchus. The West and Japan posed altogether different problems. For the latter he did not use the expression "barbarian" (*yidi*); he often referred to them with the term "four borders" (*siyi*) [namely, those living on the periphery of Chinese civilization].

As Zhang once put it in a newspaper article, this "principle [differentiating Han and barbarian] has not fallen from heaven nor has it sprouted from the earth; it did not take shape from a combination of theories, nor was it born of philosophical reasoning; we are attempting to cope with it, because it confronts us here and now."[54] This indicates one fascinating instance of the transformation of the classical, traditional consciousness of the world in China. As Onogawa Hidemi has noted, the views of Kang and Liang on Western civilization, based as they were in internationalism and central as they were to their advocacy of a Confucian religion, ultimately could not relinquish the notion that "the barbarians too shall advance to attain positions of nobility" (indeed, the barbarians would realize the essence of the classics even more splendidly). By contrast, Zhang Binglin's strict differentiation of the Han and alien ethnic groups in theory opened the way to a far more "internationalist" field of vision [because he recognized the essential differences between peoples].

Zhang's principle of strict differentiation might, of course, be extended to the nations of the West as well, for he once wrote that "there is no open pathway between Chinese and Western scholarship; although there are occasional coincidental overlaps, these are, to be sure, accidental."[56] Zhang did recognize that the West constituted a "China" on the other side of the ocean and that, together with China, Japan was a "race imbued with [correct] ritual."[57]

From time to time, the Kang-Liang group adopted an attitude that tried to synthesize all the "scientific theories" of the West with their own idiosyncratic Confucian ideas; or to regard the stunning civilization of the West as having its origins in China. From this logic it followed that there was no need to hesitate in introducing elements from the West; as the saying went, "If rituals are lost, search for them in the countryside [or the wilds]." Since they ultimately derived from China, they could not be superior to China. For Zhang this conservative argument was to be discarded, once and for all, as utter nonsense. As we shall soon see, Zhang was developing a kind of Han ethnic existentialism, an existentialism of national learning. Among the revolutionaries, at least before the 1911 Revolution, Sun Zhongshan tended to search out foreign support (from Japan and the United States) to the extent one can attribute to him a clear policy. Such a search is essentially absent from Zhang's conception of things. After the establishment of the Republic of China, Zhang actively and vociferously opposed China's taking out foreign loans.[58]

How long Zhang remained involved with *Shiwubao* remains unclear, but two years after he first joined the staff in 1896, he had certainly already dissociated himself from the reformers. Perhaps the break with the people at *Shiwubao* originated in the intellectual rivalries I have outlined. He thus had no ties to the Reform Movement, which came to life in the fall of 1898. We have already noted that he took refuge in Japan, and followed his subsequent career, including his being traced by the Qing government as a criminal for his past association with the reformist group surrounding Kang Youwei and Liang Qichao. I offer no guesses concerning the moment of transition when Zhang became a resolute revolutionary, though I shall examine his scholarship and thought once he had emerged as a revolutionary. I begin with the *Gongyang Commentary*.

We have already cited Zhang's words to the effect that "Heaven entrusted national learning to me." Originally, Zhang was a scholar who was last in a great line of orthodox development of Qing scholarship. In Zhang's case, in the process of his revolutionary activities, and especially in the process of his struggles with reformism, he effectively "recoined" Qing scholarship as "national learning" in forging his weapons of struggle. The scholarly orthodoxy of the Qing period was *kaozhengxue*, in contrast to the New Text (or Gongyang) school of the reformers. The problem comes down to Zhang's unique combination of *kaozheng* and revolution.

Of course, we should reiterate the fact that the New Text school originated in *kaozhengxue* and constituted one area within it. From around the time of the Opium War, however, the New Text school began stressing "subtle words and great meaning" as the spirit with which Confucius had imbued the *Spring and Autumn Annals*. With their slogan "knowledge for ordering the realm," New Text scholars made ferocious attacks on *kaozhengxue*. New Text learning, which originated in the Former Han dynasty, argued, as Pi Xirui (1850–1908) put it, that the "Yugong" (Tribute of King Yu, a chapter in the *Classic of History*) is the model for riparian works; the *Spring and Autumn Annals* is a collection of judicial precedents for the courtroom; and the *Shijing* (Classic of poetry) is a collection of elegant phrases for remonstrance."[59] Usefulness in bringing order to the realm was essential to this view of things.

As an example of a Gongyang scholar, we offer the case of Wei Yuan (1794–1856), author of the *Haiguo tuzhi* [Illustrated treatise on the sea kingdoms], in which he argued strongly for coastal defenses against European might. Wei enumerated the names of those brilliant scholars who were the architects of the golden age of *kaozhengxue*—men like Hui Dong (1697–1758), Dai Zhen, Duan Yucai (1735–1815), Wang Niansun (1744–1832), and Qian Daxin (1728–1804). In working hard to regularize philology and phonology, these great teachers dove into details and plumbed minute facts, and, he suggested, they might accordingly have "clogged up the wisdom of the realm, pushing it in a direction of no utility whatever." By contrast, Wei rejected the scholarship of men such as Gu Yanwu, Gu Zuyu (1624–60), Huang Zongxi, Wan Sitong (1638–1702), and Quan Zuwang (1705–55), who "did not practice classical studies, but historical studies," and who "were not men of Han learning, but of Song learning."[60]

As Kang Youwei would put it, *kaozheng* scholars read the classics, but not the spirit contained therein; they discarded and ignored Confucius's aim of bringing order to the world; and they brought her present misfortunes upon China. Kang severely attacked Gu Yanwu as the initial instigator who had led China into this adversity. "While Gu Yanwu had important accomplishments in enhancing the scholarship of our country, at the same time he became the chief offender in the destruction of our public morals."[61] Oddly, Wei Yuan raised Gu Yanwu, and Kang Youwei suppressed him; yet because Gu Yanwu's *kaozheng* work was profoundly informed by this aim of "practical application to bring order to the world," by raising Gu's case Wei Yuan may in fact have struck at the moral decay of the subsequent *kaozheng* movement. We will have more to say later about the Eastern Zhejiang school, to which Huang Zongxi, Wan Sitong, and Quan Zuwang belonged.

In the late Qing period, a sense of distrust toward *kaozhengxue* had become rather general among patriotic people devoted to reform. Indeed, even many conservative scholars were dissatisfied with *kaozhengxue* on the whole. Gradually, a marked trend developed toward combining Han learning (*kaozhengxue*) with Song learning. Eventually, Kang Youwei, Liang Qichao, and others applauded this trend by introducing and emphasizing the role played by the teachings of Wang Yangming at the time of Japan's Meiji Restoration, which became their model. The Wang Yangming school was the most radical extension of Song learning, and *kaozheng* had initially arisen directly in opposition to it. Born into a famous *kaozheng* family was the man for whom Zhang Binglin had the greatest expectations—the revolutionary scholar Liu Shipei. Even Liu diligently strove to bring harmony between *kaozheng* and the teachings of Wang Yangming.[62] Could *kaozheng*, amid this barrage of merciless criticism, preserve a rationale for its continued existence? Might it not have to link up with reform or even revolution to do so?

Kaozhengxue was "pure scholarship" (*puxue*). It was not for profit nor for fame nor for political aims. Its essential spirit was *shishi qiushi*, the search for truth (on the basis of facts) for truth's sake alone. *Kaozheng* scholars were characteristically "teachers of the classics" (*jingshi*). What was a "teacher of the classics"? As Zhang Binglin put it, generally speaking, Confucius—the man revered as the founder of Confucianism—had two aspects: as the arranger of history, the man who brought order to China's historical records and documents; and as a man engaged in educational work. The latter strain spawned the Confucian scholar (*rusheng*) whose teachings were known as the Confucian school (*rujia*); the former, by contrast, were "teachers of the classics."

Ordinarily, the Confucian scholar hung out the shingle of "practical utility" and raced about after monetary gain, a practice typical of the New Text scholars of the Former Han dynasty, according to Zhang.[63] The progenitors of the Confucian school were hypocrites and bureaucratic deadbeats. "Dressed up, they appear imposing and grand, but they act out of chicanery and deception. They swindle the sovereign above and seduce the honor of honest men below. In the *Zhongyong* [Doctrine of the mean], Confucius should have called them *guoyuan*; they are considerably worse than *xiangyuan* (in the *Analects*, Confucius said that *xiangyuan* were the "thieves of morality"). By contrast, the original duty of teachers of the classics was "to search for truth," that is, to pass on the correct exegesis of the classical texts transmitted from earlier generations and to convey it faithfully to their disciples. Although they may not have escaped denunciation as "pedants" who were ignorant of worldly affairs, they nonetheless were superior to those hypocrites who had set their minds on wealth and profit.[64]

Clearly, Zhang's view here emerged from fierce antipathy and sarcasm toward the New Text school. In this way, as Ren Fangqiu has noted, Zhang was a direct pioneer, in spite of himself, of the anti-Confucian movement of Wu Yu (1872–1949), Lu Xun, and others in the May Fourth period. His thoroughly partisan approach enabled him to arrive at more penetrating analyses of history, and this characteristic of all Zhang's scholarship enabled him to see things with a demonstrable freshness.

Yet how was it possible to link *kaozhengxue* as the learning of pedants and teachers of the classics with revolution? Zhang argued as follows: "From the time of the Duke of Zhou and Confucius until our own day, for several thousand years, political practices have changed many, many times. How can the various standards enumerated in the classics be applied today? Well, we study the classics in order to see what existed in antiquity, not in order to apply [ancient standards] today. The many works of our ancestors have been passed down to us, their descendants, and even the inferior works are still important. It is erroneous to say that these ancient books exhausted all goodness and beauty." Indeed, "the way to conceptualize antiquity is like a photograph." It is a perfectly natural emotion, he claimed, for people to revere the writings, whether good or bad, of their ancestors.[65]

It was love of the ethnic group, born of the correct knowledge of that group's history—be it beautiful, ugly, good, or evil—that mediated scholarship and revolution in Zhang Binglin's mind. Thus, for Zhang, it was the natural course of things that the more profound the revolution, the deeper one's learning; and the deeper one's knowledge, the more profound the revolution would be. Claiming that "nationalism" (*minzuzhuyi*) was the essential principle of revolution, Zhang said:

If one knows only the "righteousness" of nationalism without reading any of the histories or classics, one can never attain refined appreciation of antiquity. I believe that nationalism is much like agriculture. If you irrigate it with the people, institutions, geography, and customs recorded in the historical texts, then a thick, luxuriant growth will result. However, if you treat it only as a principle to be esteemed and fail to love the people of the nation, then it will yellow and wither away. The object of the teachings lay in history. Those who revere Confucius have abandoned the method of seeking gain and trying to administer government; they opt for the value to be found in absorption in historical facts, and they continually appreciate it. Tracing back from the *Spring and Autumn Annals*, there are Six Classics, but these Six Classics were originally Confucius's historical studies. From the *Spring and Autumn Annals* forward, the *Shiji*, *Hanshu* [History of the Former Han], and the other historical chronicles and records all [inherited] Confucius's studies of history. To hobble after the position of the Gongyang school, which looks only for the meaning of things, to laud with great spirit and vanity the theories of the "three ages" and the "three unities," and to regard all history [historical texts and historical facts] as a straw dog [namely, something useless], this is to stray far from the teachings of Confucius. Nowadays, among those advocates of irresponsible nonsense, there are those who use [Herbert] Spencer's idea that "the cat next door gave birth to a kitten" to ridicule historical scholarship.[66] But, if China is in question, who in the world lives next door? Isn't that a place where we ourselves sleep, eat, rest? Are the people, institutions, geography, and customs the cat's kittens? Aren't they in fact our living necessities, just like food, drink, clothing?[67]

It is often remarked that the New Text school looked upon the Six Classics as "sacred,"as the Bible; while the Old Text school regarded them as "history." What Zhang had to say in the long citation above accords with this characterization. Chinese authors regarded it as their responsibility to record all the "facts," and the Six Classics, in his estimation, were the written form of these factual notations.[68] To see the Six Classics as history in no way denigrated the classical texts. Rather, it was reason to honor them, for "if a nation lacks its history, the people will be cut off from their roots. . . . Without history, the essence of the people (*guoxing* [or the reason an ethnic group was who it was]) will perish, the people will lose their foundations, sink into ruination, and become barbarians."[69]

Elsewhere, Zhang noted that

among all [animal] forms with emotions and volition, only human beings are truly capable of forming societies. The most important functions of society are to build states and form ethnic groups. The indispensable elements to this end are language, customs, and history. If any one of these three elements is lacking, the sprouts of the state and the people will not be cultivated. Russia destroyed Poland and changed its language; Turkey defeated Eastern Rome and changed its customs; the

Manchus conquered China and tore its history [i.e., historical documents] to shreds. What the Manchus were trying to do was to prevent the emergence of a national anger among our people.[70]

If a nation possessed a history (namely, historical documents) for eternity, then in Zhang's view no force could destroy that nation. From the Qin dynasty through the present day, a variety of "barbarians" had invaded China and disrupted the way of the kings on several occasions, but the invaders had never been able to obliterate all the written documents of the historical record. Thus, China's recovery of independence had not proved to be all that difficult. Even if actual recovery were not attained, if the historical facts of the Chinese people's anger remained in the documents, then the hopes and aspirations for independence might await a subsequent generation.[71]

Zhang went on to compare China's situation to that of India, a nation also suffering under the oppression of an alien people. China had not fallen to the subordinate position in which India found herself: among Indians one saw scholarly decadence, customs in decline, lies shamelessly compounded, indifference to death thanks to indolence, insatiable self-interest, a lack of devotion to study thanks to idleness, flippant sycophancy, and injuries provoked by suspicion. That it had not fallen so low was, in fact, the only thing China could be happy about. One Indian man once told Zhang:

Philosophy in our nation was originally refined and superb; mathematics, too, had a tradition that extends to the present day. What we lacked was laws [that is, a political system]; so, the English came to win control over India, and those of us with knowledge of such things increased. The one regrettable thing was the utter incompleteness of our historical texts, for we lacked the means to inspire a feeling of admiration or love for our ancestors. The history of India written by the Japanese was done entirely on the basis of Western works. As a result, it confuses all propriety and can at best be termed "a history of obscenities." Thus, in recent years, university students [while overseas studying in Japan] have divided up the task among themselves and begun editing materials; they have a five-year plan in which they hope to complete a comprehensive history of India.

In other words, despite its adherents' determination, the reason the Indian independence movement had not posted satisfactory gains was that, because of a genuine lack of historical texts, the people's national consciousness was lagging.[72] Indeed, "for the independence of a national group (*minzu*), an initial study of its national essence (*guocui*) was essential. In national essence, history was the primary thing. Next to historical research, all the other scholarly disciplines were merely ordinary skills."[73]

For Zhang Binglin, Confucius's enterprise had been truly immortal. He had given the Chinese people their history, a stupendous gift to subsequent generations. The achievement of the *Spring and Autumn Annals* was many times greater than the deeds of King Yu (who allegedly brought the waters of the Yellow River under control, opened up the North China Plain, and laid the groundwork for Chinese civilization). Of course, Zhang did not praise Confucius unconditionally. It may have been the vestige of his opposition to a Confucian religion, but in certain cases Zhang did virulently attack Confucius. Under no circumstances did Zhang see Confucius as an object worthy of reverence. As for the source of Confucius's learning, Zhang argued that he was clearly a disciple of Laozi, or at least a thief of Laozi's talents.[74]

Nonetheless, Confucius "carried on the work of Laozi and disseminated the Six Classics [Laozi was supposedly a clerical official in the government of the Zhou dynasty]. He created opportunities to spread written material to the common people, and Confucius himself compiled and edited the *Spring and Autumn Annals*. It was Confucius who made known to the Chinese people the rise and fall of eras and the formation of a great civilization and tradition in China."[75] In this respect, all the noncanonical philosophers of the Zhou era were far removed from Confucius. "It is my belief that Confucius's historical compilation was no different from that of Sima Qian or Ban Gu (32–92). Only its written form was superior. In the making of tools of any craft, those who follow a model have an easy job, but those who actually create something have a hard job. Had Duke Kong [Zhang's odd appellation here for Confucius] not lived, historical writing may never have appeared in the world."[76]

But it was way off the mark to go as far as the followers of Kang Youwei and Liang Qichao had—to lose control of themselves and call for a "Confucian religion," revering Confucius as its founder. This was not the reason Confucius was the man he was. Since the dawn of history, China had been without any religion, to say nothing of a state religion.

> The nature of our people is to be attentive to political matters and to daily needs and to strive in commerce and agriculture. Our concerns do not exceed the realm of the living; we never talk about that which transcends experience. What we search for is the sanctity in ourselves. We pray to no deity as the superintendent of truth in whose service we risk our lives. The Chinese people are thoroughly secular, while the nations of Europe flatter their deities, revere their popes, and as entire nations pray to these idols. The fact that they have even institutionalized such practices is a strong indication of the great distance separating them from our sagacity.[77]

Of course, the idea that "the Six Classics are all history," well-known even in Japan since Naitō Konan lauded it, was a phrase of Zhang Xuecheng's. In fact, Zhang Binglin often drew on the work of Zhang Xuecheng. The former claimed that his "theory that the Hundred Schools and nine streams of thought [of antiquity] all derived from the officials of state"—a view for which he was later criticized by Hu Shi and which is generally regarded as a black mark on his record (although I would not necessarily agree with this assessment)—derived from the "Bibliographic Treatise" of the *Hanshu*, but he certainly inherited the idea from Zhang Xuecheng. Thus, in supporting the idea that "the Six Classics are all history," there is no doubt that he was carrying on Zhang Xuecheng's view as well.

Zhang Xuecheng went further, arguing that, "Lying between heaven and earth, all writings are the study of history (*shixue*). The Six Classics are merely the work of the Sage [Confucius] selecting six kinds of history and presenting them as moral teachings. As for the various writers whose work belonged to the *zi* and *ji* categories of books,[78] they all originated in history."[79] Zhang Binglin's views accord with the ideas expressed here. However, in this instance, Zhang Xuecheng's influence was not like ink spilled on a blank piece of paper. One should not overlook the fact that the position that "the Six Classics are all history" was a stance essentially intrinsic in *kaozhengxue* (or a stance at which it ultimately arrived).

I should add a word on Zhang Binglin's relationship to the "Eastern Zhejiang" school, for Zhang Xuecheng was celebrated as the hero of this school of historiography. Also, most of the men who had compiled the historical facts surrounding the end of the Ming era, which Zhang Binglin earnestly sought, were scholars from eastern Zhejiang, such as Wan Sitong and Quan Zuwang. On occasion, Zhang Binglin indicated his deep respect and warm feelings for Quan. Concerning Wan, he once wrote: "I once had the desire to carry on the work of Mr. Wan by collecting historical material to write a *History of the Later Ming*."[80]

It has become formulaic ever since Liang Qichao for those analyzing Zhang Binglin's scholarly filiations to point to the Eastern Zhejiang school. In discussing the roots of Zhang's thought and scholarship, Ren Fangqiu points to four important elements: (1) the philological work of the Wan (or Anhui) school beginning with Dai Zhen, passed down to the father and son, Wang Niansun and Wang Yinzhi, and passed further to Yu Yue and Sun Yirang (1848–1907); (2) Eastern Zhejiang scholarship beginning with Huang Zongxi, followed by the Wan brothers, Quan Zuwang, Zhang Xuecheng, and others, and coming down to Huang Yizhou (1828–99); (3) Indian philosophy (Buddhism); and (4) Western philosophy. Ren notes that while he took particular account of the Eastern Zhejiang school, Zhang effectively lumped all four groups together and applied his own distinctive yardsticks (ethnic thought and democratic thought), criteria clearly based on his own scholarly approaches. In counting Western philosophy among the roots of Zhang's thought and democracy as one of Zhang's personal yardsticks, Ren points to Zhang's frequent mention of such thinkers as Kant, Schopenhauer, Spencer, and Nietzsche.

While this was one of the reasons Zhang was once scorned by Japanese scholars as having only superficial knowledge, it does not mean that he picked up his ideas from these Western thinkers.

Furthermore, we might affirm here what has been denied to Zhang. After all, his notion of "democracy" was a forerunner of May Fourth period thought; he pointed to a belief in equality as an achievement of Confucius; and it was he who first called for a "republic" while working with the overseas students in Japan and the group supporting Sun Zhongshan. Yet we need not place the word "yardstick" beside "nationalism." Zhang's enthusiastic advocacy of *lisu* (rites and customs) and his esteem for *chunfeng meisu* (pristine customs and practices) seem rather far removed from our own ideas of democracy, or what Qian Mu has referred to as "populism" (*pingminzhuyi*).

These two points aside, Ren's thesis fits Zhang well. In developing his ideas on Eastern Zhejiang scholarship, Ren sees three areas of influence on Zhang Binglin: (1) that aspect of the Eastern Zhejiang school stressing historiography, in which the thought of Zhang Xuecheng particularly excelled; (2) the fact that Eastern Zhejiang historiography was an ethnic, nationalist historiography; and (3) the belief in the unity of theory and practice, philosophy and praxis. Although Zhang Xuecheng had already forcefully pointed out the third of these three, apparently Ren found it superfluous to mention that Zhang Binglin inherited it from this source. In short, Ren Fangqiu's ideas seem reasonable enough. Yet, I think we ought to consider just how Zhang himself actually looked at the Eastern Zhejiang school. In the fourth section of his work *Jianlun*, we find an essay by Zhang entitled "Qing ru" (Qing Confucians), in which he has the following to say:

The Eastern Zhejiang school emerged in the late Ming period. The brothers Wan Sida (1633–83) and Wan Sitong of Yin [the county in which Ningbo is located], with Huang Zongxi of Yuyao as their teacher, studied and emphasized ritual, though at this time they selected their ideas from a mixture of both Han learning and Song learning. Furthermore, Wan Sitong particularly emphasized historical theory. Continuing in this line was Shao Jinhan (1743–96) of Yuyao and Quan Zuwang of Yin, both of whom were skilled in historical research. Zhang Xuecheng of Kuaiji wrote the *Wenshi tongyi* and the *Jiaozhou tongyi* [General principles of bibliography], and he revived the scholarship of

Liu Xin and Ban Gu. The brilliance and foresight of his observations approach those of the *Shitong* [by Liu Zhiji]. In addition, scholarly study of ritual never ceased. While carrying on the traditions of the Eastern Zhejiang school, Huang Shisan (1789–1862) of Dinghai made the initial contacts with the Wan school [namely, the philology of Dai Zhen and others]. His son, Huang Yizhou, authored the *Lishu tonggu* [A comprehensive explanation of works on ritual] and brought to completion his research on the ritual systems of the Three Dynasties [Xia, Shang, and Zhou] of high antiquity. One might say that the scholarly groups along the upper reaches [namely, the Wan school] and the lower reaches [namely, the Eastern Zhejiang school] of the Zhe River [lit., Zhejiang, but here referring to the Fuchun and Qiantang rivers] were formed in this way.[81]

Thus when Zhang Binglin spoke of the Eastern Zhejiang school, he was combining historiography with studies of ritual institutions. In uniting these two with the philological and phonological work of the Wan or Anhui school, he saw this as the completion of Qing scholarship. In the time Zhang spent at the Gujing Jingshe, he often met with Huang Yizhou and questioned him about scholarly matters. Also, in the article cited above on Qing Confucian scholarship, Zhang listed Sun Yirang, whom he revered even more than his own teacher Yu Yue, as the most extraordinary philologist of the Anhui school, not of the Eastern Zhejiang school, even though in terms of place of origin Sun was a native of Ruian, in eastern Zhejiang province. He was the author of the major work *Zhouli zhengyi* (The true meaning of the rites of Zhou), in 86 *juan*.

When one says that Zhang was influenced by the Eastern Zhejiang school, it is best to see three principal elements in this influence: a nationalist historiography, the view that "the Six Classics are all history," which was an established formula among scholars of this school; and studies of ritual institutions. These defined the scholarly topography of the territory of Zhang Binglin.[82] Zhang may have fancied that the orthodox lineage of *kaozhengxue* would come to grief when he said: "I am confident that *protecting popular morality with philology and phonology* does not contradict my honorable teacher [Yu Yue], nor does it run counter to my teacher [Sun Yirang]. Although everyone may obstinately continue to hold that this is a departure, I shall not back down."[83] Yet by the same token, he worked hard to master Eastern Zhejiang historiography and studies of ritual institutions (this would include the *Tongzhi* of Zheng Qiao and the *Wenxian tongkao* of Ma Duanlin)—the very items that Wei Yuan of the Gongyang school once firmly set himself against as philology and phonology; Zhang also studied the work of the *zhuzi* from the late-Zhou era.

It was probably the overall trend in *kaozhengxue* that extended the object of philological-phonological analysis from the classics to the *zhuzi*, and a number of famous works in this vein appeared in succession: *Zhuzi pingyi* (Critical discussion of the *zhuzi*) by Yu Yue, *Mozi xiangu* (Analysis of the *Mozi*) by Sun Yirang, and *Xunzi jijie* (Collected explanations of the *Xunzi*) by Wang Xianqian (1842–1918). In this regard, Zhang too continued the orthodox *kaozheng* lineage. In general terms, what constituted Zhang's scholarly terrain was a union of classical research (the orthodoxy for the three centuries of the Qing dynasty), philology, historiography (with the Eastern Zhejiang school's special approach), and studies of ritual institutions, as well as such newly arisen areas of research as *zhuzi* studies and Buddhism. What one must note in this context is the point that it is not entirely appropriate to call this exclusively *kaozhengxue* or Confucian documentary scholarship. For the reasons already outlined, I see the idea that "the Six Classics are all history" as the necessary culmination of *kaozhengxue*.

As is generally known, *kaozhengxue* arose in opposition to the philosophy of nature and principle (*xinglixue*) of the Song and Ming dynasties. However, *kaozhengxue* and *xinglixue* shared the premise that the classics of the sages were sacrosanct. A "classic" (*jing*) was not simply a written text that recorded "facts"(*shi*). It also expressed the "way" (*dao*) of doing things or the "significance" or "righteousness" (*yi*) of events. The school of nature and principle understood in a straightforward manner the *dao* recorded in the classics by the sages and sought to realize it through practice. By contrast, the *kaozheng* school began with a correct intellectual understanding of facts, while an explanation of the *dao* residing within those facts and the practical applications it necessitated were, as it were, placed within parentheses, to be anticipated at a later date. The former was unconcerned with an objective "method" for comprehending the *dao* inherent within the classics. The latter persisted in honing the techniques of its "method" to the point of neglecting its aim, and ultimately, as it tried to see the classics solely as "source material," the inevitable result was emotional paralysis.

In any event, this was the philosophical view that had come naturally to be demanded of *kaozhengxue*—namely, Zhang Xuecheng's thesis that "the Six Classics are all history," the view that the six *jing* were records of *shi*. Of course, Zhang Xuecheng's thesis argued for the unity of *shi* and *dao* from the perspective of *shi* or facts, for it was not a simple belief in facts for their own sake. Rather, it was a profound philosophy of *kaozhengxue* that simultaneously transcended *kaozhengxue*. Zhang Binglin took this position to a radical extreme, to the point of virtually assuming a stance of pursuing facts for their own sake. At work here was Zhang's characteristically thoroughgoing attack on the New Text reformism of Kang Youwei and Liang Qichao, in keeping with the overall trend of that era; for the Western impact had raised considerable doubts among Chinese scholars about the traditional *dao* itself and had necessitated a separation of *shi* and *dao*.

The group surrounding Kang and Liang continued to advocate the "way" of the sages and the establishment of a Confucian religion. Even they were compelled to argue, in stipulating the content of this "way," that it contained "progress," "universal truths," and "popular rights." The "classics," in which according to Zhang Xuechang the "sages" had ensconced the *dao* in "facts" (*shi*), were merely the record of those "facts," according to Zhang Binglin.[84] And for the very reason that the classics recorded "facts," the "rites and customs" of the "Chinese people," they deserved esteem. Zhang Binglin never tired of emphasizing that this point was beyond the shadow of a doubt, as would the later work of Gu Jiegang (1893–1980) and Qian Xuantong.[85]

Furthermore, while this view of Zhang's was a continuation of the *kaozheng* tradition, it also clearly far transcended the boundaries of a simple *kaozheng* empiricism. To be sure, this was *kaozhengxue* in methodology only, for ultimately we cannot call it *kaozhengxue* of historical reality. *Kaozhengxue* had traditionally assumed the existence of the sages and was predicated on the moral absolutism of the classics.

This point will become clearer when we consider Zhang's studies of the *zhuzi* philosophers. Among his many achievements was a pioneering effort in contemporary studies of the *zhuzi*. His work in this area includes various essays in his *Jianlun* (which contains a number of pieces that revised views put forward earlier in his *Qiushu*) and his "Zhuzi xueshuo lüe" (Outlines of the theories of the *zhuzi*). In these writings, Zhang restored Confucianism and Confucius to a place among the "nine streams of thought and Hundred Schools" of antiquity.

Nowadays, and for those of us who are not Chinese, it is difficult to sense the acuity of Zhang's perception in this instance, but we must recognize the meaning of what he had done. Over the long period of two thousand years from the Han dynasty on, Confucianism alone was orthodoxy, while the *zhuzi* were either considered heterodox or at most supplementary material for the Chinese intellectual tradition. As a result of the development of this orthodoxy itself—namely, as a result of *kaozhengxue*, the final pinnacle of this development—the Chinese intellectual tradition negated itself and returned completely to its origins. For Zhang the tradition was not exclusively *kaozhengxue*, nor was it solely Confucianism. It was all "national learning" (*guoxue*). The age was one in which the reformism of Kang and Liang, who sought to save the nation by remaining within the bounds of Confucianism—even with the doctrine of a "Confucian religion" outfitted with its own ideas of liberty, popular rights, constitutionalism, progress, and the like—could not, in the final analysis, achieve this ultimate aim.

Two elements are missing from Zhang's concept of national learning, as outlined thus far: Neo-Confucianism and literature. Neo-Confucianism's absence is perfectly understandable for

Zhang Binglin as a *kaozheng* scholar. However, one advertisement in *Minbao* (issue no. 8) for the "Society for the Revival of National Learning" (led by Zhang) gives a lecture schedule of six items: *zhuzi* studies, the writing of history, the study of institutions, the study of the Buddhist canon, Song and Ming Neo-Confucianism, and Chinese history. In fact, from just after the 1911 Revolution onward, Zhang often expressed his own distinctive ideas about Neo-Confucianism. As for literature, early on he had written essays such as "Wenxue lun lüe" (A short essay on literature).[86] Also, as is evident from the inclusion of the study of Buddhist texts in the advertisement just cited, Buddhism, too, was for a time considered within the scope of "national learning."[87]

When was Zhang's idea of "national learning" born? As an idea it first emerges clearly in his "Yuzhong ziji" (Prison diary), and it probably began to take concrete shape in prison. While he was incarcerated, some like-minded scholars began publishing *Guocui xuebao* (Journal of national essence), a revolutionary journal specializing in national learning (Feng Xunlun, who served in the Chinese government in the 1950's, and his friends wrote many scholarly and political articles for it); this publication undoubtedly exerted a great influence on Zhang, and vice versa.

In Japan, "national learning" (*kokugaku*, the Japanese reading of the Chinese characters for *guoxue*) arose in opposition to "Chinese learning" (*Kangaku*) there. Zhang Binglin and his comrades advocated "national learning" (which they also referred to as "national essence") in opposition to European scholarship. This point is readily apparent from the introductory essay in the inaugural issue of *Guocui xuebao*. There one reads the following citation: "Miyake Yūjirō [Setsurei, 1860–1945] and Shiga Shigetaka [1863–1927] established a journal and called for the preservation of the national essence." China, however, had a tradition of continuous scholarship covering several thousand years, a scholarly tradition structured around classics, histories, philosophical works, and literature. It encompassed more than just the subtleties of metaphysics, extending to the actual implementation of administrative science. In such a magnificent country, the appearance of an advocacy of national learning or national essence is a matter of course, an assertion of deserved rights, and under no circumstances is it reasonable to denounce this movement as reactionary.

Whereas Westerners often express their opinions in the name of religion, anyone who has ever read a Chinese text realizes that the Chinese invoke "scholarship" (*xue*) for the same purpose. Furthermore, from its inception in China, national learning militantly aimed at the clear political objective of a nationalist revolution. As the first issue of *Guocui xuebao* put it, "We study the learning of all the countries of the world, East and West, not objectively, but subjectively, with the aim of restoration."[88] There is a healthy nationalist position in this statement. Scholarly opinion in Europe at the time was diametrically opposed to this sort of "national essence," and Zhang was attentive to this trend as it made its way gradually eastward.

Because national independence had already been achieved in Europe and Japan, the search for meaning in their national essence leads either to invading other countries or to treating others as slaves or drones. Hence, intelligent men [there] are angered by this and fully oppose [the idea of] "national essence." They must adopt such a point of view if they wish to correct such abuses. However, this does not apply in the cases of China and India. For thieves to destroy the writings of great thieves and bandits of the past would be a glorious event, but it would be entirely absurd to try and do the same to good families.[89]

For Zhang, the position of strictly distinguishing the self from the other [we and they], a principle of logic (well demonstrated in the work of ancient logicians), tempered by philology and Buddhism, and a thorough attack on the reformism of New Text Confucianism, which drew continually on the examples of Europe and Japan, further radicalized the concept of national essence. Without wishing to gloss over the beauty or ugliness of Chinese civilization or scholarship as a whole, Zhang argued, what a truly marvelous thing it would be to study the feelings "passed on to descendants through the books in the libraries of their predecessors."[90]

The case of Japanese civilization and scholarship, virtually all of which is borrowed from elsewhere, scarcely deserved Zhang's attention. He thought it the utmost disgrace that the reformers continually held up Japan as an example. To say that a philosophy of "practicality" such as that of the Wang Yangming school proved efficacious in Japan's Meiji Restoration was tantamount to saying that Japan's civilization was genuinely superficial. Thus, Japan's enlightenment had come late, for just a decade earlier Japan had finally managed to dispense with feudalism. Clearly, few among the Japanese people had been subjected to the poison of civilization, he argued, and their national character was well protected in its simplicity.[91]

We can see just how shallow Japanese scholarship really is, Zhang argued, by the extent to which the Japanese adopted Chinese learning, while at the same time none of them had fundamentally mastered the study of ritual.[92] Japanese professors and scholars were not the senders of letters but the mailmen; and their students were the recipients of this mail. Chinese students in Japan had to overcome their rampant Japanophilia.[93] What Zhang most liked in Japan seems to have been Japanese clothing and the convenience of obtaining Buddhist texts.

Zhang was not nearly so harsh on European scholarship, nor did he absolutely refuse to accept European superiority in certain areas. He basically saw Western scholarly systems of thought as qualitatively different, the product of a different race. Were the Chinese to swallow Western culture whole without regard for their own history and scholarship, it might lead to the advocacy in all seriousness of such laughable anachronisms as constitutionalism. Constitutional or parliamentary government was appropriate only in Europe or Japan, where feudalism had been overcome only after lasting well into modern times. For a people like the Chinese who had passed that historical stage long ago, this was certainly not something to be hoped for.[94]

As far as Zhang was concerned, the only country in Asia, aside from China, that had an indigenous high scholarly level and could genuinely call itself a civilized nation was India. It had earned his attention because only India had in the past exerted a profound intellectual influence on China. To be sure, the depth and perceptiveness of Indian philosophy (principally Buddhism) could not ultimately approach the highest expressions of Chinese philosophy, such as that found in the *Zhuangzi*. And, as we have seen, India lacked historical studies and a science of government. China was unique in the world with her systems of political thought and studies of ritual ever since the Duke of Zhou had compiled the *Zhouli* and with her historiography ever since Confucius's *Spring and Autumn Annals*. Also, the philosophy of Weishi Buddhism, the essence of Indian philosophy, had already been absorbed by the Chinese and transformed into a native entity. Nor could one even imagine that the indigenous Chinese philosophical systems of the *zhuzi* might be outdone by Westerners. Could the Han race, with such a magnificent civilization and intellectual tradition, go on suffering under the rule of wild beasts like the Manchus?

We have now laid out the relationship between revolution and national learning in Zhang Binglin's thought. Liang Qichao once noted that "Zhang did not extend his view beyond his own gate," i.e., China. Zhang's national learning was deeply permeated by an opposition to the New Text school of reformers. This carried with it opposition to constitutionalism and parliamentary government as well as to evolutionism; in addition to ridicule of Japan, it meant exaltation of pure, textual scholarship and disdain for the salaciousness of the political world surrounding scholars; and it pointed to the danger inherent in the reformers' position that "democracy" would serve as a model to be followed as in the West (or, as Mao Zedong once said, "I sought truth in the West"). In contrast, Zhang saw all this as "imperialism." He vilified Huang Zongxi, "pioneer of democracy in China," as a disgrace; and he ridiculed Wang Yangming—who was counted even by the *Guocui xuebao* as one of the three sages to be taken as a model— as a hellish demon (*raksha, yaksha*). For all these reasons and more, Zhang had to base himself in the principle of thoroughgoing revolution supported by his particular partisan consciousness.

Zhang's exaggerations here, his irrational arguments (which have been noted by Ojima Sukema),[95] and his idiosyncratic ideas have been pointed out in the past. We need not belabor the unfairness of his view of Japan and the injustice of his critiques of Huang Zongxi and Wang Yangming. Similarly, in arguing for a school of learning distinctive to China, he was no match for the New Text school, with that school's appeal of a "scientific theory" and capacity to stimulate a climate for democracy. By the same token, he was no match for Sun Zhongshan's insights and awareness of the times and saw Sun as merely amassing a bunch of Western theories. After becoming enamored of Weishi Buddhism, especially while in prison and during the *Minbao* period of his heyday as a revolutionary, Zhang published many articles of a heavily Buddhist cast, so much so that they were once satirized: "*Minbao* should speak for the voice of the people, not the voice of Buddhism."

In developing his ideas, which have been called nihilistic by Ojima Sukema and Onogawa Hidemi, and in linking them to a theory of violent revolution, Zhang's writings took on an odd (at times, even desperate) tone.[96] At the same time, there surfaced a firm moralism and anti-utilitarianism, as can be seen in his "Geming daode lun" (Argument for revolutionary morality). All this was perfectly natural for a man of such self-sacrificing devotion as Zhang, who as a scholar professed his entire life to be a proponent of textual criticism, and who as a revolutionary pursued a revolution in the sense we have described it here. In a word, he could not avoid being kept at a distance by his fellow revolutionaries. When Ma Xulun visited Zhang in 1911, just before the revolution, Zhang was living in obscurity in a small house in a suburb of Tokyo. He told Ma that he was feeling extremely homesick.[97]

Zhang Binglin and Indian Independence

The article by Zhang that follows ("Ji Yindu Xipoqi wang jinianhui shi") was carried in the editorial column of *Minbao* (no. 13 [May 5, 1907], pp. 93–97). Its most striking quality for Zhang the revolutionary is his demonstration of deep concern and sympathy for the fate of India and her independence movement. He wrote a number of subsequent pieces for *Minbao* (through issue no. 20) that concerned India.[98] That *Minbao* began with issue 21 to carry news of the Indian independence movement was undoubtedly thanks to Zhang's supportive articles. India had been a cause of profound concern for late-Qing radicals because of her devastating sufferings at European hands. Reformers and radicals alike shared the anxiety that China *not follow in the footsteps of India*. However, it would be no exaggeration to say that, although many essays would be written about how India had to become independent and remain so well into the future, and about how China had to align with India so they could finally defend Asia against white imperialism, at least before the 1911 Revolution Zhang Binglin was alone in arguing along these lines.

Zhang's early pieces for *Shiwubao* expressed a kind of Pan-Asian consciousness. Although this seemed to die down for a time, it reappeared in his work together with his interest in Buddhism and India. Furthermore, this position did not emerge from some opportunistic, tactical concern for a revolution, nor was it an empty "Asianism"; it developed from a profound sense of respect and affection for Indian scholarship and the Indian people who had given birth to it. (Zhang had tried to study Sanskrit while he was in Japan, and when he was later in prison he made plans to travel to India.)

Before the 1911 Revolution, Kang Youwei had often raised the example of India as convincing proof that revolution was impossible. When he was forced to flee abroad following the failure of the 1898 Reform Movement, Kang lived as a guest (perhaps for as long as eighteen months) at a government office in India. It was from this period of personal observation that his views took shape: "Many Japanese writings claim that in the future India will be independent. I, however, would assert that that day is not likely ever to come unless the English were to completely disappear from Europe and several hundred George Washingtons were to be born."[99] Zhang's response was that one would do what one had to do, but this is a fairly silly argument, lacking any substantiation and largely advanced by Zhang, it would seem, for rhetorical purposes. Nonetheless, which side has history ultimately proved correct?[100]

An Account of the Commemorative Meeting for Shivājī of India

On April 20 [1907] the Indian students here [in Japan] convened this meeting to commemorate Shivājī [1627–80] at the Toranomon Women's Hall [in Tokyo]. The master of ceremonies was a lawyer by the name of Mr. A.

Mr. A had come [to Japan] from the United States, and he visited me at the *Minbao* editorial offices. He said: "The treatment meted out to Indians by the British government was far worse than that of the Mogul dynasty of earlier times. Those who set their minds on learning have been unable to study politics and law, and, even if they go overseas to pursue their studies, they still feel under a strict prohibition in this area. Only in America was I free to study, and I finally earned a law degree there." He granted this interview with the interpreting help of his friend, Mr. B, who speaks Japanese quite well. When both gentlemen spoke of the decrepit state of India, they broke down in tears as their strong feelings welled up.[101]

I asked about the contemporary state of the Indian national association. They responded: "Only because it actually existed was it a source of consolation to the public spirit." They compared this to the Greco-Roman revival in Europe, and they regarded China and Japan as fraternal nations. In the area of learning, they were well-versed in the strong and weak points of Buddhism, Vedanta, and modern Western philosophy. They also demonstrated a thorough knowledge of such Chinese [philosophers] as Confucius, Laozi, Zhuangzi, Zhu Xi, and Wang Yangming. Furthermore, they felt sorry that China had lacked a Wang Yangming school in recent times. Indeed, these were enraged, indignant, heartfelt men from India.

At the end of the seventeenth century, Shivājī arose among the populace, overthrew the Mogul empire, and brought independence to the Indian people; in these ways, he was comparable to Ming Taizu in China. Nowadays the Indians do not boast to the masses that they will dare oppose England and plan for their independence, but they have all come to this commemorative meeting to make their intentions known. When they understand how Shivājī opposed the Moguls, they will then comprehend that they must defy England now. The people who attended this meeting all felt this way in their hearts and agreed with this objective. Even if they could not agree on the appropriate path to take, there was no reason for them to try to obstruct it.

Mr. A had already invited me and several other comrades to attend the meeting. Several hundred Japanese were in attendance, and among them Ōkuma [Shigenobu] addressed the audience warmly. When he arrived at the door in his expensive carriage, the band played animatedly and with inspiration; the audience did not grieve for the demise of India but clapped their hands for Ōkuma. When Ōkuma saw that there were British gentlemen and ladies in attendance, he shook hands with them respectfully and showed great humility before them. I never thought Ōkuma, being such a famous politician, would act like that.

In his speech, Ōkuma said: "That the English crown has taken such good care of India was an act of sympathy and generosity—nothing can compare with it." In encouraging the Indians, he urged social reform and cautioned against bearing resentment toward others or planning riots. A certain Englishman followed him at the podium. He generally said that Englishmen and Indians were as close as flesh and blood. He spoke smoothly with all possible cajolery, probably because he knew in his heart of the kindness and generosity of the Indian people. Accordingly, he tried to entice them. We need say no more about him. What we should be suspicious of is the fact that even Ōkuma, this "Oriental hero," still tries to flatter. Has he become senile? Are all his energies dessicated? In the first place, perhaps he wants to get the Indians to lend a hand because of the [Anglo-Japanese] Alliance. On the part of political office holders and leaders of the opposition parties, this is the way things should be. But, Ōkuma has already retired from politics and has no relationship to state policy. And yet, he made this speech. I really do not understand this.

When Mr. A first visited me, he said: "A thousand years ago

there were Indian monks who, together with Japanese monks, came to China. Chinese monks stopped them and let them stay with them; and they [the Chinese monks] said: 'Are not our three countries like a folding fan? India is the paper; China is the bamboo frame; and Japan is the pivot linking these two to the handle. Even if the pivot is small, it is this point that guides the handle. Now, both the paper and the bamboo frame are torn asunder, and only the pivot increases its good deeds from day to day. The pivot must cooperate with the others.' " Alas, what hopes lay in these words for Japan!

China and Japan have both revered the Buddhism of India and enhanced its morality, playing much the same role as Greece did for the modern European countries. When the Greek nation had already perished, the English poet Byron helped in its [fight for] independence. Is this any different from the place India occupies for our two countries [China and Japan]? Of course, China is in no position to plan even for itself at present, but Japan can still offer some vague hope. Even if [Japan] cannot extend its administrative or military strategies that far, the will must remain alive.

The Indians are an extremely peaceful and gentle people. They are benevolent, trust others, and easily soothe others with kind words. Even if someone is an enemy, they will reconcile once they shake hands and their anger is released. Fortunately, even if one or two scholars are aroused to rage, they would represent a lonely voice and suffer for the fact that they would be so few in number. They [the Indians] speak secretly and dare not speak their minds. Even at the very edge of humiliation, still they do not speak of the pain in their hearts. Although this meeting sang the national anthem with bell and drum throughout, this is no different from the way, in days gone by, the followers of Tian Heng dared not cry as they sang the Haoli.[102] Finally, their indignation drove others to speak on their behalf. Now Ōkuma, learning from this example, is trying to make himself their spokesman. How can we remain indifferent to this?

If it was a matter of his being among Englishmen and not wanting to betray his real feelings, then all he [Ōkuma] had to say was: Be faithful to your motherland and strike when the iron is hot. Why does he mention love for the English throne? The way the English treat the Indian people is indeed somewhat better than the way the French treat the Vietnamese. However, one can tell that to the Vietnamese people, but to do so to the Indians would be a big mistake. The nomadic Moguls, smelling of goats and sheep, treated the Indians in a much more easy-going fashion than do the English today.

We should know that the more civilization advances, the more it tramples humanity under foot. It has already taken our children and destroyed our homes. Furthermore, this is like regarding a little charity as [genuine] benevolence and regarding the good treatment of prisoners as virtuous. Generally speaking, the civilized countries clog up people's eyes and ears with false morality. The French treat the Vietnamese people like domesticated animals; the English treat the Indians like beggars. Although beggars may be a bit better off than oxen and horses, what do you do with the fact that all their rights are gone? India today is just one giant orphanage. There should be no honorable man of will who could observe its state and not shed tears and become distraught. The story of [Lord] Byron penning the military anthem of Greek independence should have genuine utility for India today. Ah, though Byron was an aristocrat, he was still a young poet with no experience in great undertakings. Compare him to those great men who helped their sovereigns in the great task of realizing his mandate in the establishment of a state, and his reputation and career cannot, of course, match theirs. Will the present world never be witness to a single Eastern Byron?

Mr. A has entertained the notion of visiting China. I told him: "The officials of the Qing dynasty were like blubber, like chamois leather, looking out only for their own advantage. Even if you are a man of culture and learning, they will regard you as a barbarian from a dying land." True enough, but speaking from the present perspective, the politician's way of thinking can be generally understood.

Pondering this further, Ōkuma said, using the cases of Canada's and Australia's gaining their autonomy, that India could do so as well. This is truly an invidious comparison. Autonomy in

Australia was given primarily to the English, not to the native population. Autonomy in Canada was given to Englishmen and other Caucasians, not to the native population. Even if the British government were to release India to independence, the blessing would be bestowed only on the white men. Even if the Indian people and the American Indian population are not really comparable, the former have been generally better treated. Take the American black man, who, although he possesses the franchise in name, is in fact not the equal of other citizens. He cannot escape being lynched and burned at the stake (both under the banner of capital punishment). How much more valuable a resource are the Indians for the British? Do you think the kingdom of Great Britain will make common cause with the Indian people?

The Filipinos have obtained the right to elect representatives because they resisted with force. However, the Indians gave their lives for the British and devastated the Transvaal. That was the most extreme act. The Transvaal has gained autonomy, but the Indians still do not have their independence. Thus, there is no comparison with the Philippines. Talk of "kindness and magnanimity" is merely an effort to vindicate the English and force the Indians into a trap. This is tantamount to stopping the crying of children by enticing them with some candy. It is deception of the worst kind.

We supplement this piece with two passages along similar lines from other articles by Zhang on India.

Ōkuma Shigenobu, the man without principles from Japan, once gave a speech on Asia. Chinese and Indians came to listen. Ōkuma said the following: "Among the civilized nations of Asia, Japan is first and China is second. Although countries like Babylonia and India may be seen as cultures of bygone days, now one cannot compare them with these [Japan and China]." . . . Observing culture while harboring a sycophantic heart must always be resisted. Once India can gain its independence and win victory over England, her level of culture will not necessarily be any higher than it was the day before. I think that if Ōkuma had heard this said, he would change his argument. There are people who are arrogant and those who are vulgar. Here [in the case of Ōkuma] are combined both arrogance and vulgarity. If a good doctor were to examine his nervous system, I wonder what it would look like. . . .

One Indian man said: "Before Japan had arisen, there were at times minor disturbances among the nations of Asia, but it was still close to being peaceful. This has now been reversed. . . . Who was it who flattered the white man and ridiculed his own kind?!"[103]

*   *   *

The magical arts of China came initially from India, before they crossed the sea to the East and arrived ultimately in Japan. All [three peoples] believe in compassion and fairness. From ancient times forward, India has never once invaded another country. Although China and Japan have governed more widely, in treating the conquered peoples they have not lost their humanity and committed outrages to the extent that Europeans have. . . .

In the political art of ruling a country, although China may one day prove superior to India, China can never approach India in the latter's principle of universal love for all things. Should our two countries some day help each other and enable all our people to find their places, then, without trampling another nation under foot or killing one another, we can make the gang of imperialist thieves feel profound shame. Looking equally upon all the red and black races living on our borders will be the duty of our two nations as pioneers. This is, needless to say, something timeless, not something to be anticipated within a definite time period. Many people today, though, plan for the short run. It has been said that China is in decline, and it will be hard for her to revive, while India will forever be sinking into ruin. Why have we no perspective on the long run?[104]

Confucius in the
Era of the 1911 Revolution

I would like to begin this essay by spelling out three underlying premises: (1) China was a Confucian country for two thousand years, from the time Confucianism was made the state's educational orthodoxy by Emperor Wu of the Han (r. 140–86 B.C.E.) through the collapse of the Qing dynasty in 1911; (2) Confucius was the supreme personality in Confucianism, which is to say that Confucianism meant the teachings of Confucius; and (3) for those two thousand years, neither Confucianism nor Confucius was ever subjected to any fundamental undermining. With these three points as established facts, I hope to put aside any controversy that might arise about them for now and proceed with the issue at hand.

Of course, one can easily imagine different arguments. For instance, one could argue that calling China a Confucian state speaks only to superficialities, that in fact what gave order to the daily lives of the Chinese people was either Daoism or, at the least, Daoistic beliefs. This view has been forcefully stated by such scholars as Tachibana Shiraki (1881–1945). Another perspective, in the political realm, argues that although decked out in an ostensibly Confucian ideology, the genuine machinations of Chinese politics were most often fully permeated by Legalist realism. This view, as once argued by Ojima Sukema (1881–1966), is perfectly reasonable as well.

Yet another stance questions the position of Confucius himself. It divides this period of two thousand years in half and argues that in the first half, the thousand years from the Han through the end of the Tang, the supreme personality of Confucianism was not Confucius but the Duke of Zhou. The Duke of Zhou was enshrined as a "sage of antiquity," while Confucius was enshrined as a "teacher of antiquity." Confucius was seen as the propounder of the Way of the Duke of Zhou, as his assistant.

This too has become a popular point of view. However, I would just note that the state rituals built around Confucius as sage are far too numerous to spell out.

Confucianism and Anti-Confucianism in Modern Chinese History

The history of Confucianism may be seen as a history through which the position of Confucius increasingly moves toward center stage. Hence the decisive step was that taken by Song scholars. From the Song period on, the facts that the highest status in human history belonged to Confucius and that "Confucianism" meant the teachings of no one but Confucius himself became widely, unshakably, accepted. For now, though, I will round off the numbers and accept that Confucius was considered the supreme personality for the entire two-thousand-year period. That he occupied this position in the field of education is an indisputable fact.

There are, to be sure, differences of opinion surrounding Confucius and his teachings, but these differences do not touch on the foregoing "widely accepted" points. Suffice it to say that no debate has arisen which questions the dignity of Confucius as a sage per se. From the Song dynasty on, the image of Confucianism was recast as the "learning of the Way" (*daoxue*); although the textual critical school (*kaozhengxue*) of the Qing opposed the Song school, the image of Confucius remained unshaken. To be sure, the criticism made of Confucianism in the Ming dynasty by Li Zhi (Li Zhuowu) enormously rattled the traditional image of Confucius, but ultimately it was Li Zhi who retreated.

As one contemporary Chinese text puts it:

The anti-Confucianism of the Taipings late in the Qing period and their opposition to Confucius himself were truly unprecedented. When the leader of the Taiping peasant revolution, Hong Xiuquan (1813–64), set the revolution in motion, he overturned the mortuary tablets of Confucius with a dauntless revolutionary spirit. He declared that the feudal emperor [of the Qing] was the "King of Hell," and claimed that "in searching for the origins of the mysterious acts committed by evil spirits, we ultimately return to the fact that the books of the teachings of Confucius are full of errors." The way of Confucius and Mencius supports feudal control, and its unvarnished reactionary nature does harm to the working people. Furthermore, stories circulated that the revolutionary peasantry of the Taipings beat Confucius in the courts of the Heavenly Kingdom and, as punishment, ordered him to work as a farmhand in their vegetable gardens. Such was their intense scorn for Confucius. The Taiping revolutionary army raised high the anti-Confucian banner. They "arrogantly dared to call Confucius and Mencius devils and to burn the [Confucian] classics, histories, and prose writings all day long." Wherever he was lionized, they destroyed the images of Confucius, burned Confucian temples to the ground, denounced the Confucian Four Books and Five Classics as "the devil's books and heretical theories," and ordered that these books "be completely incinerated and forbade anyone to read them."[1]

This was not the anti-Confucianism of individuals. It was implemented as authorized policy through administrative institutions.

Be that as it may, the Taipings' denunciations of Confucius were merely the mad instructions of ignorant "bandits" who were "led astray by the heterodoxy of a barbarian religion." Also, the Taiping Rebellion lasted for only about fifteen years. By no means can one accept it as fact that the Taipings' anti-Confucianism, as well as their antipathy to Confucius, deeply permeated the consciousness of the common people and retained its power to influence them. At least one cannot accept as fact that anti-Confucianism was the principle fueling nationalist revolution prior to 1911, or for that matter at the time of the May Fourth Movement.[2] Such an argument is ultimately no more than a bad dream.

In recent years, a thoroughgoing attack or denunciation of Confucius and Confucianism was carried out as "state policy" in the PRC, completely engulfing the masses of the Chinese people (led by the masses?), with the anti-Confucius, anti–Lin Biao campaign. Indeed, this campaign occasionally recalled the Taiping Rebellion, but (as Zhou Enlai pointed out early on), it would probably be correct to conclude that this campaign was less directly a continuation of the Taiping Rebellion than a link to the anti-Confucian element of the New Culture Movement of the May Fourth period and to the efforts to bring down "Confucius and Sons."[3] The anti-Confucianism of the May Fourth Movement clearly differed in nature and hence in its roots from that of the Taipings, which derived from the exclusivity of their belief in Christianity.

Why did such an anti-Confucianism arise simultaneously with the May Fourth Movement? When and how were the positions of Confucianism and Confucius first undermined? In what follows, I would like to offer one historical perspective on this issue. Furthermore, in part as a corrective to the unexpected raising of this issue solely from the angle of class struggle in the recent anti-Confucius campaign in China, I would like to analyze it instead in terms of the development intrinsic to the subject itself—traditional Chinese intellectual history, which is to say in this context the history of Confucianism. For in a country such as China, in which native systems of immense learning have continually appeared and evolved, I believe such a perspective to be absolutely essential. I start from the assumption that the three points raised in the opening paragraph are accepted.

Three Views of Confucius in Qing Scholarship

First, learning or scholarship in the Qing period was, in a word, textual criticism or *kaozhengxue*. Although the actual content of "textual criticism" was multifaceted, its core lay in the Confucian canon, namely empirical studies of the classics. The sanctity of the classics as well as the unique supremacy of Confucianism, which is to say the sanctity of Confucius, was an indubitable, immovable premise. On this basis, *kaozhengxue* was first and foremost the search for truth on the basis of facts (*shishi qiushi*), and trusting only that which was based upon proof. More than anything, it was a study of methodology; it demanded the search for substantiation, for evidence.

Evidence for classical textual criticism, of course, had to be sought within the classics themselves; that is to say, substantiation of the classics was achieved through the classics. It was an inevitable further step to draw citations from the writings of the noncanonical thinkers of antiquity (the *zhuzi*) as the documentary evidence temporally closest to the composition of the classics. In this manner, the *zhuzi* themselves came under scrutiny and ultimately came to be studied for their own intrinsic qualities. Thus they were seen not merely as the source of citations for classical philology; as intellectual texts with their own distinctive content, the works of the *zhuzi* came to be recognized anew, and study of the writings of the *zhuzi* was revived after two thousand years of neglect. Hence, this is doubtless the logical chain of events behind the revival of *zhuzi* studies in the late-Qing period.

While this point of view is certainly not incorrect, an even greater role was in fact played by the development of bibliographic science, itself the inevitable product of the development of *kaozhengxue*. The recognition that "If one were unfamiliar with the 'Bibliographic Treatise' of the *Hanshu* (History of the [Former] Han Dynasty), one could not read the books of the realm" was universal. In any event, the writings of the *zhuzi* were revived as the scholarship of an original group of thinkers who stood apart from the Confucians. Of course this is not to say that Confucianism, its sanctity never having been doubted, became relativized. However, fundamentally contained within *kaozhengxue* was the tendency to "see the classics and the Way as two entities,"[4] and the logical end of this line of reasoning was that Confucianism—i.e., Confucian scholarship or learning— was just one stream of thought ("the Confucian school") of the original "Hundred Schools and nine streams" listed in the "Bibliographic Treatise" of the *Hanshu*. In short, Confucius was no more than one of the *zhuzi*.

The earliest argument along these lines can be found in the Qianlong period (1736–95) in the "Moxue tonglun" (A complete analysis of the learning of Mozi, 1792) by Wang Zhong (1745– 94). In this essay, Wang pointed out clearly that Confucius and Mozi had been contemporaries of comparable stature, and that, were one to discuss them evenhandedly, there was just as much justification for analyzing the thought of Mozi as there was for analyzing the thought of Confucius. For his efforts, one of Wang's contemporaries vilified him for "crimes against orthodox moral teachings."[5]

Needless to say, *zhuzi* studies did not proceed along a smooth, straight path. Yet there was no going back, as can be seen in the work of Chen Li (or Chen Dongshu, 1810–82), *Dongshu dushu ji* (Dongshu's reading notes on the classics, 1879), which found it impossible to ignore the writings of the *zhuzi*. Clearly, from the middle of the nineteenth century forward, one must take into account the influx of Western thought as a powerful indirect stimulus for the revival of *zhuzi* studies. This was, however, only a secondary catalytic element. The trend toward a revival of *zhuzi* studies in the Qing period and hence the demotion of Confucius to the ranks of the *zhuzi* must be seen first and foremost as a consequence of Qing *kaozhengxue* itself.

Second, as Liang Qichao (1873–1929) pointed out, it was basic to the main thrust of *kaozhengxue* (which is to say, Chinese classical studies) that it provided the impetus to go further and further back in time in search of antiquity. The ceaseless pursuit by *kaozhengxue* of the authentic face of the classics was a search for knowledge of the era temporally closest to those classics; and, as the search moved further back in time, it inevitably went beyond Zheng Xuan's (127–200) classical scholarship before arriving at the period of the Former Han. Classical studies in the Former Han were primarily of the New Text school, the core of which was the *Gongyang Commentary* on the *Spring and Autumn Annals*, which, it was claimed, had been "discovered."[6]

It was of course entirely possible in this instance that New Text classicism was being interpreted solely with the philological textual methods of *kaozhengxue*—as, for example, in the case of Kong Guangsen's (1752–86) *Chunqiu Gongyang tongyi* (The comprehensive meaning of the *Gongyang Commentary* on the *Spring and Autumn Annals*). One need only recognize here the distinctive quality of classical studies of the New Text school. The central idea of New Text classicism and in particular of the *Gongyang Commentary* was "subtle words and great meaning" (*weiyan dayi*); the *Commentary* was considered to be brimming with "remarkably bizarre points of view and marvelous ideas." The image of Confucius in these writings was one of extraordinary mysteriousness, with a prophetic, even religious, quality. A religious image of Confucius had long existed in China, but its emergence as an essential element of organized classical learning was a phenomenon unseen until the Qing era.

Especially after the Song dynasty, the image of Confucius, be it in the Neo-Confucian school of principle (*lixue* or *xinglixue*) or in *kaozhengxue*, was one of an entirely rational Confucius who would not discuss the supernatural [a paraphrase from the *Analects*]. In fact, it was this very point that Chinese literati always proudly flaunted when they had contact with Christianity. Furthermore, what New Text classicism discovered, as the development of Qing scholarship came to a close, was a mysterious, prophetic, religious Confucius born into the world by virtue of the spiritual powers of the Black Emperor [one of the mythical five emperors of highest antiquity].[7] Thus, in spite of itself, *kaozhengxue* of the Qing period struck upon two entire unexpected conceptions of Confucius: Confucius as merely one of the *zhuzi*, and Confucius as a figure of mysterious, religious qualities.

Third, the two points made thus far concern the images of Confucius that emerged as an inevitable result of Qing scholarship. As was pointed out, though, in addition to the internal Chinese causes for the change in the image of Confucius at the end of the Qing, one must also include the so-called impact of the West as an extrinsic reason. The first response at the time that Western culture and Western thought began to reach China late in the Qing period, particularly after the Opium War, was opposition and resistance. The Chinese response in the Ming period to Western culture and religion brought by the Jesuits was startlingly different: a mixture of indifference and odd curiosity. In the late-Qing case, the Chinese were compelled to recognize the actual predominance of the West. A smooth acceptance of such a situation is not something a self-respecting civilized nation can concede. Indeed, while coming to recognize this supremacy, in order to discount its value, so to speak, the theory was developed and advanced that "We already had that [i.e., what seems to make the other superior] in antiquity"; and in order to temporize in a situation in which the inevitable had to be accepted, the notion that "when the rituals are lost, seek them in the countryside" was invoked.

Simultaneously, texts were being extracted from the whole body of past Chinese learning to use as rivals and opponents to every area of Western scholarship and thought. The situation was sufficiently critical for the response not to be limited solely to the classics of Confucianism. Although the *zhuzi* thinkers were not seen as inherent in the Chinese tradition, as quasi-native entities they and even Buddhism could be mobilized for the cause. Physics and geometry, of which the West was so proud, were successfully discovered to have had their original principles set forth several thousand years earlier in the work of Mozi.[8] The secrets of political science, it was argued, had been put forward by Xunzi and Hanfeizi. Were the philosophies of Kant and Hegel, of which the West proudly boasted, ultimately superior to the profound philosophy of Buddhism?[9]

Leaving aside Buddhism for the moment, we note that an altogether new recognition had come into existence: the era of the *zhuzi* or Hundred Schools of antiquity was now seen as a Golden Age in Chinese scholarship and thought. Freedom of thought, the very womb of Western civilization, was now found to have existed, majestically, in China as well. For the "School of Nature and Principle" of the Song and Ming periods—namely, the schools of Zhu Xi (1130–1200) and Wang Yangming (1472–1528)—the era of the *zhuzi* had been one in which heterodox ideas ran rampant, obscuring to a great extent the correct teachings of Confucius and Mencius; it was seen as a dark age, when human passions had inundated the world and individuals merrily pursued their arbitrary points of view. In the heyday of *kaozheng-xue*, the writings of the *zhuzi* had been, in the final analysis, merely the source of auxiliary documentation, and the *zi* [author of an individual *zhuzi* work] was at most "an accessory to the classics." Now, however, this era was transformed into a Golden Age in which the Hundred Schools of thought were in intellectual contention, the most radiant period for the freedom of thought in all Chinese history. The *zhuzi* were now described as thinkers who developed constructive, innovative ideas on a par with all Europe's "scientific principles."

The problem was not whether or not China had had anything comparable to (modern) Western systems of thought. The point was: Who in the world had extinguished the once brilliant radiance that had flourished in China?[10] Of all the *zhuzi*, the most radiant was Confucius. It was Confucius who was the enlightened, pioneering thinker of his day. And so the image of a conservative Confucius, teacher of the School of the Way, was changed to that of an enlightenment figure, a progressive, egalitarian Confucius.

I have discussed here the three new images of Confucius that *kaozhengxue* fostered in the Qing era.[11] While this was a historical development, it was a logical one as well. These three views of Confucius were synthesized by Kang Youwei, and in the Reform Movement of 1898 what emerged was the monolithic advocacy of a Confucian religion.

The 1898 Reformers: Kang Youwei and the Advocacy of Confucianism as a Religion

In 1891 Kang Youwei, the leader of the New Text school, wrote his famous book *Xinxue weijing kao* (A study of the forged classics of the Xin period). In it he proclaimed the earth-shattering thesis that the Ancient Script (Old Text) editions of the classics, the standard texts for *kaozhengxue* throughout the Qing period, were by no means the authentic Confucian classics; that Liu Xin (53? B.C.E.–23 C.E.) had forged them to legitimize the Xin dynasty of usurper Wang Mang (45 B.C.E.–23 C.E.); that Zheng Xuan had given these editions further currency; and that they all had merely twisted and perverted the true traditions of the teachings of Confucius. And he offered "textual proof" of the orthodox authenticity of the New Text editions of the classics.

Later, apart from his famous 1895 Memorial of Provincial Graduates (*gongche shangshu*) [opposing China's acceptance of peace terms following the Sino-Japanese War], Kang published a second book, *Kongzi gaizhi kao* (A study of Confucius as a reformer of institutions) in 1897. *Kongzi gaizhi kao* was by no means just a textual exegesis of the classics. It was at the same time a work laying the groundwork for the political stances of the New Text (or Gongyang) group and outlining the *zhuzi* thinkers' systems of thought. The essential ideas of Kang Youwei's reformism can be found in full in these two books of his, especially the latter, *Kongzi gaizhi kao*.

The first chapter of this work begins with "An Analysis of the Fact that Antiquity Must Not Be Vaguely Investigated." In the second chapter, "An Analysis of the Successive Rise of the *Zhuzi* and the Establishment of Their Teachings at the End of the Zhou Era," Kang wrote:

Humanity was born from the Great Flood [an idea associated with the biblical Noah's flood]; the people of the world were all born at the time of King Yu of the Xia [who was famous for bringing flood waters under control]. For the two thousand years that followed, their numbers increased, their knowledge grew, and they came to be fully endowed with reason. Brilliant men emerged one after the other, and, by virtue of nature and circumstance, set their minds on establishing theories, amassing followers, reforming institutions, and setting forth standards [racking their brains to create new political structures].

Yet, swayed by the alternating spirits of *yin* and *yang* that they had inherited, they could only produce incomplete theories; and they could do no more than clarify their own principles. Furthermore, they each traveled and endured hardship alone, as they spouted their profound and beautiful views. They followed their convictions undaunted, seeking to establish their doctrines and spread them throughout the realm (to form a world order on the basis of their own principles).

At this time, the Buddha, Brahmana, and the 96 pagans all created their doctrines in India; Zoroaster developed his new teachings in Persia; and Greek culture reached its apogee with the emergence of the seven wise men and the compilation of the teachings of Socrates in the West. The appearance of the various religions of the world flourished during the Spring and Autumn and Warring States periods [in China]. The outcome of the thriving situation of the *zhuzi* was that the public returned to the most inspired of them all, who completed a great unification and ultimately set the standard for all subsequent generations. In the *Lun-heng* [Disquisition, by Wang Chong, 25–97? C.E.], he is called Confucius, and he is dubbed "eminence of the *zhuzi*." This is indeed correct. All the people in the realm believed in Confucius and his great Way was achieved. Thus, after the Han there were no more *zhuzi*. I would like now to look at the *zhuzi* of the Spring and Autumn and Warring States eras, men who established scholarly followings, be they famous or virtually unknown.

Finding it unnecessary to discuss Mozi, the Daoists, or the Legalists, Kang proceeded to give an overview of the establishment of various other schools of thought, examining the written documents of each in detail. These schools included those of Zisang Bozi, Yuan Rang, Shao Zhengmao, and Chen Zhongzi. The third chapter of *Kongzi gaizhi kao*, following the same procedure, examines the fact that the *zhuzi* founded their schools of thought in order to effect institutional reforms or reestablish political institutions. Kang's book reached its climax in Chapters Eight ("An Analysis of the Fact that Confucius Was a King who Created Laws") and Nine ("An Analysis of the Reason Confucius Established Confucianism for Institutional Reform").

There is no need to review the Reform Movement of Kang Youwei, Liang Qichao, and others. In this area, I yield to the many reference works and scholarly studies, first among them Onogawa Hidemi's *Shinmatsu seiji shisō kenkyū* (Studies in late-Qing political thought). What I would like to turn to and offer an analysis of here is one of Kang Youwei's memorials, introduced and sanctioned as the gist of the reform policy at the time the reformers gained the ear of the regime in power and reformist political policies commenced. This is the memorial of the sixth month of the 24th year of the Guangxu reign (1898). Although political approval in China was attained through the Emperor, in most cases it was officially announced by means of the imperial sanction of a memorial from a subject. Thus, this memorial was tantamount to an imperial policy decision, an order to be executed. The memorial itself combined the three views of Confucius current in the late Qing that I have described. It also provided the starting point and the model for arguments over a Confucian religion that would become a major issue in the Chinese intellectual and political worlds of the Republican period.[12]

The memorial contained the following lengthy title: "A Memorial Submitted for Imperial Inspection and Respectfully Presenting the Author's *Kongzi gaizhi kao*, *Xinxue weijing kao*, and *Chunqiu Dongshi xue* (Mr. Dong [Zhongshu's] study of the *Spring and Autumn Annals*), Requesting the Establishment of a State Ministry of Religion and Churches as well as Employment of Confucius's Birth for Dating and Permission to Have Confucian Churches Among the Populace, and Furthermore the Abolition of Prayer to Deities Unworthy of Reverence so as to Stress a National Religion, and I Respectfully Implore and Pray that the Imperial Glance Be Directed upon the Above Items." When Kang came to explain the content of the memorial, he expressed thanks for being allowed to submit to the Guangxu Emperor as reference material on political reform several additional works of his own: *Riben Mingzhi bianfa kao* (A study of the political reforms of Japan under the Meiji Emperor), *E da Bide bianzheng zhi* (A record of the institutional reforms of Peter the Great of Russia), *Tujie shoujiu xiaoruo ji* (A record of the conservatism and decay of Turkey), *Bolan fenmie ji* (A record of the partition and fall of Poland), and *Faguo geming ji* (A record of the French Revolution). Then, after making the prefatory comment that, since all these books just describe "techniques of statecraft" and do not touch on the "essential point concerning religion," he again offered the three works mentioned in the title. And then, on the basis of all the foregoing, Kang entered directly into the issue of a Confucian religion.

In an introductory section, Kang described in enormous detail how polytheistic practices were still rampant in China at the time and how superstitions underlying sacrificial rites were the shame of the nation. He then proceeded to examine the cause of all this. Although in the past there had been ceremonies for Confucius, he noted, only the lower-level educational officials and students (the *shengyuan*) were allowed to participate in them. *The common people, women, and children were not permitted to take part in the services.* It was this point that had to be scrutinized, for if the Chinese people, high and low, did not worship Confucius, then China would be unable to avoid the scorn of Europe and America. By praying to a single "religious founder" as was done in the West, China too would be able to unify her people's minds, and that "religious founder" had perforce to be Confucius. In this connection Kang offered three points of substantiation.

First, at the end of the Zhou period, the *zhuzi* arose one after the other, each establishing his own doctrines and proposing institutional reform. Although Confucius was but one of these *zhuzi*, he was the most brilliant of them ("the eminence of the *zhuzi*"). Confucius *wrote* the Six Classics as a means of effecting institutional reform. The common view that Confucius "transmitted but did not write" the classics was false. He was an uncrowned king, a religious founder. In other words, according to Kang Youwei, he was an "uncrowned king" in the sense that he conceived institutions for a dynastic house that was to follow the Zhou. And he was a religious founder in the sense that he possessed the religious quality of "having been born into the world as a result of contact with the spiritual powers of the Black Emperor." He was never simply an erudite and profound scholar.

The *zhuzi* at this time, such as Laozi and Mozi, all sought to become religious founders and to develop their ideas for political reforms, but each of them made only one-sided proposals. The teachings of Confucius were the most comprehensive and universal, for he was superior to all the other *zhuzi* in that he approached humanity's feelings with the Golden Mean. He was not merely greater than all the past *zhuzi*, but superior to all foreign religious founders as well. The founders of religion in Europe and elsewhere all relied on the Way of their deities (miraculous deeds), only then earning the people's faith in them. Confucius, by contrast, did not depend upon the pathway set by a deity; he was the one and only sage capable of becoming a religious founder. Thus, Kang concluded, the likes of Confucius had never before been seen in the world: a genuine "religious founder for a civilized world." The essence of his teachings (institutional reform) and his program for it were to be found entirely within the text of the *Spring and Autumn Annals*, and the correct understanding of the *Spring and Autumn Annals* could be known only through the *Gongyang zhuan* or *Gongyang Commentary*. In other words, Confucius had been born miraculously, "religiously," but what he propounded in his teachings was thoroughly "civilized" and this-worldly.

Second, Kang argued, the present era was clearly different from the olden days when rulership and religion had been unified. In the present, an international society had already taken shape. Whereas Confucius had created "principles for the realm" and "principles for clans," the modern world was one of "principles for the nation" or nationalism. Thus, one could not necessarily implement the teachings of Confucius without change. "Rites become important according to the age" ("Liqi," in *Liji* or *Book of Rites*). With appropriately selective implementation, there would be no reason to violate the teachings of Confucius.

Third, since rulership and religion had followed divergent paths, Kang continued, this by all means required special officials for Confucian doctrine. China had to establish a state Ministry of Religion (*jiaobu*) at the center and churches in the localities; and as a means of dating, China should use the birth of Confucius as the starting point. The institutions of a Ministry of Religion and churches would be regulated, and there would be Confucian temples built at every level of Chinese society from the capital to the provinces, the prefectures, the counties, and the townships. Confucius would be made the equal of Heaven (perhaps as God was in Christianity), and all the people, men and women alike, would be encouraged to worship him.[13] With the founding of a Confucian church in every town and village, someone conversant in the Four Books and Six Classics would be named Lecturer (*jiangsheng*), and this person would discourse on the sage's classics every seventh day, a day of rest. A head of Confucian churches throughout the country was to be appointed Minister (*shangshu*) in the Ministry of Religion of the central government. Furthermore, all the schools of the land would fall under the supervision of the Ministry of Religion.

The position Kang was advocating here was a call for the recognition of "freedom of religious worship," a view that must have been difficult to understand at the time, but it was a view fully consistent with his "movement for a Confucian religion" in the Republican period. In any event, these are the general contours of Kang's 1898 memorial calling for the establishment of a Confucian religion as a state religion.

Kang's advocacy of these points can already be seen clearly in his famous Memorial of Provincial Graduates of 1895.[14] We have not mentioned here the measures taken toward evangelizing a Confucian religion overseas (especially in Southeast Asia), nor detailed the various differences between these and his later proposals for a Confucian religion. Be that as it may, there is no doubt that Kang's starting point with regard to the principles of a Confucian religion lay in the role played by religion (namely, Christianity) in the formation of the wealthy and powerful nations of Europe.[15] In a certain sense, these instances from the experience of the West may have been accepted as a "law" for the "modernization" of the non-European world. One can see throughout the work of Zhang Binglin that he for one continually rejected acceptance of the European case as "law," maintaining a strict differentiation between Europe and China. (See, for example, the speech, translated in full [in the previous essay], he made at a meeting held in his honor in Tokyo when he arrived in Japan following his release from prison, particularly where he talks about religion.)

The image of Confucius as a religious founder upheld by the supporters of a Confucian religion was, of course, entirely different from his image in the earlier Confucian tradition. As Liang Qichao later wrote, the true nature of the teachings of Confucius, which Kang Youwei had done so much to clarify, lay in the fact that they were progressive, not conservative, egalitarian, not authoritarian, sharing, not self-righteous, strong of character, not frivolous, and spiritual, not hedonistic. Indeed, this was an enlightened Confucius, an enlightenment Confucianism, and nothing else.[16] As Liang would put it, Kang Youwei had set his mind on becoming the "Martin Luther of a Confucian religion," or so he hoped.

Let me now lay out several issues inherent in this discussion.

First, the essence of Kang's program was a longing for the formation of a "nation." In the Republican period, the movement for a Confucian religion clearly had a reactionary character to it, but at this stage—a stage when the Revolution of 1911 was not yet the order of the day (the manifesto of Sun Zhongshan's Xing Zhonghui [Arise China Society] had yet to attract any sort of response on Chinese soil), a stage when British, French, German, and Japanese imperialist aggression was advancing unchecked—one would have to say that it had a rather more progressive than reactionary thrust. This was the groping toward and emergence of a desire to create a nationalist core by lumping into a single group all the Chinese people—who had been seen as "a sheet of sand" or sharply divided between officials and commoners—in order to bring into existence a stable and secure solidarity.

Second, we should note that Kang's conception was of a Confucian religion from above, religious unity from above. Religion here was not of a fundamentally different dimension than the state or politics; it was conceived as something to be circumscribed within the parameters of the government or its administrative apparatus. This inclination to insist that the Confucian religion always be tied to state power became rapidly apparent in the Republican period. Although the view that the Reform Movement of Kang Youwei, Liang Qichao, and others constituted the first step in bourgeois reformism is an influential perspective, what we have seen here is closer to a traditional Chinese bureaucratic concept of the state than to a "bourgeois" concept.

The third point I would like to make is that, even though Confucianism was tenaciously promoted as a "religion," it was not a religion of salvation in the sense we are likely to conceive of religion today. Rather, it was simply a "doctrine" (*jiao*). Just after the 1911 Revolution, when the movement for a Confucian religion was first put forward as a movement, one of the key figures, Chen Huanzhang (1864–1938), attacked opposition to the term "Confucian religion" (*Kongjiao*). He felt that "the Way of Confucius" (*Kongdao*) was nothing more than a theoretical concept, and the expression "Confucian learning" (*Kongxue*) was too narrow. Only the term "Confucian religion" was sufficiently all-inclusive. "Initially the Chinese character *jiao* contained the three senses of religion, education, and moral teaching, and *Kongjiao* [the *jiao* of Confucius] combines these three. This is the reason that *Kongjiao* is great. However, although it is endowed with these three qualities, ultimately religion lies at its foundation."[17] In short, it is best to think of "Confucian religion" as resembling the combination of the Imperial Rescript on Education and prayers at the Ise Shrine in prewar Japan, which silently forged a national religion while coexisting with formal freedom of religion.

In this article by Chen, the clarion call of a movement for a Confucian religion, neither of the central qualities of movements in modern Chinese history—namely, anti-feudalism and anti-imperialism—emerges in any clear form. If one considers Confucian religion itself "feudalistic," then advocacy of a Confucian religion will, needless to say, probably be feudalistic rather than anti-feudalistic. However, would it be rash to argue, as did Tan Sitong, the reverent disciple of Kang Youwei and fervent supporter of the principles of a Confucian religion, in his *Renxue* (On benevolence), that if one is looking for anti-imperialism pure and simple, support for a Confucian religion will lead one directly to feudalism itself? This idea is pregnant with all sorts of possibilities.

Kang Youwei's most faithful disciple and the trailblazer of Chinese journalism was Liang Qichao. In a sense Liang was even more active than Kang, and just as fervent an advocate of a Confucian religion as his teacher. In 1897, before the 1898 Reform Movement, he had called out—as item ten in the "School Regulations of the Shiwu Academy of Hunan"—the need to spread to all nations Confucius's teachings of peace and great harmony. The "School Regulations" comprised ten sections altogether: (1) Setting the mind to work; (2) Cultivating the mental faculties; (3) Regulating the body; (4) Reading books; (5) Studying principles; (6) Learning culture; (7) Enjoying one's fellows; (8) Maintaining hygiene; (9) Administering the realm; and (10) Spreading the faith. The first eight of these were school regulations, and the last two were for after graduation. Thus, the Shiwu Academy of Hunan was an institute aimed at nurturing human talent for the purpose of administering the state and propagating the faith. Item ten, "Spreading the faith," read as follows:

No. 10. Spreading the faith. The feeble and sad present situation concerning our sage's teachings. There are 400,000,000 people who are said to have accepted these teachings. Excluding the half of them who are women, half of the remaining half who are illiterate, 60–70 percent of the rest who are merchants and low-level functionaries, and 80–90 percent of the remainder who were base scholars who only know how to prepare for the imperial examinations, and you are left with a situation Zhuangzi accurately summed up as follows: " 'The whole state of Lu is dressed in Confucian garb!' said Duke Ai. . . . Zhuangzi said: 'In the whole state of Lu, then, there is only one man who is a real Confucian.' "[18] In addition, foreign theories[19] are running rampant, being pushed and proselytized everywhere, with an unmatched vehemence protected by the influence of state power. Alas, if we fail to think about protecting ourselves today, the destruction of our teachings will be at hand. Our aim in founding this academy is to establish a principle based on reverence for Confucius. [Confucius's disciple] Zigong said: "No one who is not let in by the gate can know the beauty and wealth of the palace that, with its ancestral temple, its hundred ministrants, lies hidden within."[20]

The reason Westerners think our doctrine so superficial and vulgar scholars personally ridicule our teachings lies in their failure to understand the true reason why Confucius was a sage. We have to make this clear by drawing out for detailed examination on the basis of recent events the principles, institutions, subtle words, and great meanings of the Six Classics. Then, the true face of Confucius, as a model for all generations whose morality shall blanket the entire world, shall emerge. Two citations from the *Analects* of Confucius: "The master wanted to settle among the Nine Barbarians of the East"; and he said: "I shall get upon a raft and float out to sea."[21] After all, the teachings of Confucius were not merely for the governing of one state, but for the governance of the entire realm. Thus, it says [in the *Doctrine of the Mean*]: "His fame overspreads the Middle Kingdom and extends to all barbarous tribes. . . . All who have blood and breath unfeignedly honor and love him."[22]

On the day when you complete your studies [here] and graduate, it is our great desire that the final point of your studies will be spreading to all nations of the world Confucius's teachings of peace and great harmony. The task of "spreading the faith" belongs to the period following the completion of studies. Because the schoolwork at this academy all centers on the principle of glorifying the sage's doctrine, this last assignment may in fact be called the task of "spreading the faith."[23]

"The point of greatest contrast between [Liang] Qichao and Kang Youwei," wrote Liang just a few years later, "is that the latter had too many fixed ideas and the former too few."[24] In this way, Liang, ardent follower of a Confucian religion, changed his views remarkably and retreated from the fray. In 1902, when Liang was a refugee in Japan, he wrote "Baojiao fei suoyi zun Kong lun" (Protecting the faith is no way to honor Confucius), in which he expressed his new point of view.[25] "This essay differs from essays written several years earlier. That is to say, I am now turning my sword on myself." He claimed effectively here that he had once been a valiant general in the party fighting to protect the faith, but now he had become its enemy. "Do not accuse me of being fickle," he argued, "for I love Confucius while I love truth even more. I love my elder colleagues and friends, but I love freedom even more. By overturning an established view of the past two thousand years and declaring war on 400,000,000 people, I seek to repay the favor of Confucius, the favors of various founders of doctrines, and the favor of the people of the nation." Later in this essay, he wrote:

Those who over the past ten years have lamented the state of the contemporary world have unfurled the tricolor banner calling for the protection of the nation, protection of the race, and protection of the faith, and they have been calling for these things as they run around the nation. I too was a foot soldier marching beneath such a banner. However, in scrutinizing the overall situation with our present mental and visual powers, we must henceforth devote our energies only to protecting the nation, for protecting the race and the faith are not as critical. The reason for this in the case of "protecting the race" is that the distinction here is unclear: does it mean protecting the yellow race or protecting the "Chinese" (*Zhonghua*) race? If it means protecting the yellow race, then Japan also belongs to the yellow race. Japan is at present a rapidly rising nation, and it hardly needs our protection. If this expression implies protecting the "Chinese" race, our 400,000,000 people occupy one-third of the entire globe, and I do not believe that they will be completely destroyed even if they are enslaved. If we are able to protect the nation, the race will naturally become stronger than before. Hence, protecting the race falls within the scope of protecting the nation, and there is no particular need to use the expression "protect the race."

He then proceeded to the next point: "As for the notion of protecting the faith, let me summarize four points for why we can forgo it. (1) 'Protecting the faith' fails to reveal the true face of Confucius. (2) It fails to have religious significance. (3) It fails to anticipate future changes in religion. (4) It fails to recognize the connection between religion and politics among the Powers." From here, Liang offered more details on these points.

Nonetheless, the "Confucian religion" cannot be obliterated. The Confucian religion can never die out, for it hangs from the sun and moon in the sky, it fills the atmosphere of heaven and earth. Other doctrines lay emphasis on ceremonies, but when freedom prospers, ceremonies die out. If they are based in superstition, as truth becomes clearer, superstition will become obsolete. That these two points are absolutely incompatible with the civilization of the future shines with the certainty of a universal law of progress.

The Confucian religion, however, is qualitatively different from other religions. Confucius taught the reason why human beings are human, why human society is human society, and why the state exists as such. The more civilization progresses, the more study of his teachings will be required. Many of the great educators of modern times have advocated education for character-building, but none of those wise sages—then or now, East or West—has analyzed human character to the extent Confucius did. In the area of moral education in the world of the future, Confucius will truly occupy the most important position. What Confucius expected of us was surely not for us to dub him a savior or become the object of prayer. Neither Socrates nor Aristotle can come anywhere near Confucius. If there should ever arrive an age in the world when politics, education, and philosophy cease to exist, perhaps the Confucian religion would die out; but, as long as these three exist, the glory of a Confucian religion will never disappear. Those who wish to protect the faith may sleep in peace.

My fidelity to a "Confucian religion" lies elsewhere. It lies in allowing our Confucian religion to flourish and mature by opening its doors without limitations, by expanding its terrain, and by inviting many doctrines to join us. All religions that direct their faith toward a pantheon lack the magnanimity to include the doctrinal principles of other religions. But this is not the case with [the teachings of] Confucius: "If even a simple peasant comes in all sincerity and asks me a question, I am ready to thrash the matter out, with all its pros and cons, to the very end"; "The master said, 'Even when walking in a party of no more than three, I can always be certain of learning from those I am with.' "[26] The spirit of a Confucian religion is not authoritarian; it is one of freedom. We honor Confucius because we must carry on this spirit and not let it cling tightly to its past. [As Mencius wrote:] "Among the sages, Confucius was the most timely one."[27] If Confucius were to be born today, there would certainly be elements of his doctrine that he would alter.

Liang published this essay of 1902 in the journal *Xinmin congbao* (No. 2), just three years after he had written "Nanhai Kang xiansheng zhuan" (A biography of Mr. Kang [Youwei] of Nanhai) and "Lun Zhina zongjiao gaige" (On religious reform in China). Probably his contact in Japan with the "scientific theories" of the contemporaneous European variety gave rise to this enormous undermining of his earlier views on protecting the faith. Subsequently, Liang scarcely touched on "Confucian religion," save in obligatory situations, in personal relations, or in passing mention when the main point of religion was absent.[28]

Kang Youwei, however, stuck to his support of a Confucian religion to the bitter end. Once he embarked on the life of a refugee, though, traveling virtually everywhere throughout the world, the crucial element for which he sought support became his movement for the "protection of the emperor." In the end, the movement for a Confucian religion, as a movement, broke up after the 1898 Reforms, before the formation of the Republic of China. Let me still make one incidental point, though. Slogans such as "great unity" and "the realm is for all" made it possible for the principles of a Confucian religion, the essence of the 1898 Reform Movement, to spread throughout China, and they were originally slogans of the reformers of New Text classical learning. These slogans were inherited by the revolutionaries, in particular by Sun Zhongshan.

The Revolutionaries: Opposition to a Confucian Religion by
Zhang Binglin and Other Nationalists

Although Sun Zhongshan issued the manifesto of the Xing
Zhonghui, the first public call for revolution in China, in 1894
(in Hawaii) and 1895 (in Hong Kong), it has become virtually an
established thesis that the revolutionary movement in the
Chinese hinterland began only after the Boxer Uprising of 1900.
It had to wait for the central figures at the time—Sun Zhongshan,
leader of the overall movement; Huang Xing, the man responsible for the military uprising; and Zhang Binglin, the man in
charge of propaganda—to forge a decisive bond of cooperation
with the founding of the Tongmenghui (Revolutionary Alliance)
in 1905. Putting aside the transition to this revolutionary movement for a moment, I would like to examine how Confucius was
dealt with by the "revolutionaries" following the Boxer Uprising.

One can scarcely find a critique of Confucianism or of Confucius in Sun Zhongshan's work at the time. Years later, in his
speeches of 1924 on the "Three Principles of the People," he
called for the "kingly way" (*wangdao*). He also offered high praise
for certain ideas found in the text of the *Daxue* (Great Learning),
such as "cultivating one's person," "ordering the family," "ruling the state well," and "bringing peace to the realm," and he
argued that they formed the finest political philosophy in the
world. Furthermore, his emphasis on the political ideals of "great
unity" (*datong*) and "the realm belongs to all the people" (*tianxia
wei gong*) makes inordinately clear his high assessment of the
teachings of Confucianism or Confucius as a national heritage.[29]

In the period prior to 1911, however, Sun's views were considerably less clear. Actually, prior to his 1924 speeches on the
"Three Principles of the People," Sun had articulated no clear position on Confucianism or Confucius. Rather, he had assumed
the clear-cut attitude of a nationalist revolutionary who early on

had had contact with European culture and hence was not thoroughly immersed from childhood in Chinese learning.[30] Still, it would probably be appropriate to acknowledge that Sun had the ordinary or even more than ordinary respect for Confucianism as a national heritage and Confucius as a great man.

In creating a propitious atmosphere for the revolutionary movement, the two most energetic pamphleteers were Zou Rong (1885–1905) and Chen Tianhua (1875–1905). None of their writings express any distinctive view of Confucius, save according him the traditional respect. In his last testament, Chen Tianhua wrote: "If religion must by all means exist, then the veneration of a Confucian religion as we have seen it heretofore would seem to present no problem. If we want to avoid acting contrary to custom, then reverence for Buddhism too would be acceptable. Christianity is fine insofar as it honors freedom, but to transform it into a national religion for this reason alone would be going too far."[31] This is one example of his mentioning the issue of a national religion.

Even in the propagandistic writings of the revolution, for example, such as the regulations of the Longhuahui (a secret society), there is a strikingly frank emphasis on Confucius and Mencius as sages who called for rebellion against tyranny and particularly against rule by an alien race.[32] Drawing on the words of Confucius to try to establish a basis for rebellion, nationalism, and democracy was not unheard of among the revolutionaries. This stance, though, does not seem appropriately singled out as a distinctive view of Confucius held by the revolutionaries. The most noteworthy view of Confucius among the revolutionaries was that held by Zhang Binglin.

Zhang Binglin was a most fervent revolutionary. He was also the last great teacher of textual scholarship (*kaozhengxue*) in the Qing period. And he was a formidable scholar, who brought a comprehensive synthesis to Qing scholarship and recoined the expression "national learning."[33] In particular, he opposed Kang Youwei, Liang Qichao, and the other reformers and responded to their assaults with ferocious counterattacks from the revolutionaries' position. His meritorious service in propagating the righteous cause of nationalist revolution would earn him immortality, as he himself was wont to boast.

Zhang's revolutionary thought was closely linked to his scholarly learning. In other words, although we described earlier how the New Text school emerged as the last product of *kaozhengxue*, the New Text school both grew out of *kaozhengxue* and transcended it. From the perspective of orthodox *kaozhengxue*, it was a kind of devil that had come to advocate a rather bizarre and incredibly self-indulgent philosophy. By contrast, most scholars did not agree with the New Text school and sought to follow the orthodox path of *kaozhengxue* with documentary textual methods. Thus, it was from among these scholars, successors to Qing orthodox *kaozhengxue*, that Zhang Binglin finally emerged as scholar and intellectual.

Zhang Binglin's distinctive approach to scholarship and knowledge first appeared in his book *Qiushu* (Book of persecutions). There are two editions of the *Qiushu*, a new and an old one. The old edition was published either in 1900 or 1901, but the articles in it were all written prior to July 1900. The new edition of the *Qiushu* took many of the articles from the earlier edition, revised some of them considerably, dropped a few entire essays, and added some new ones. It was published in Tokyo in 1904. After the publication of the new edition of the *Qiushu*, Zhang virtually ignored the older edition with its strong reformist orientation; whenever he referred to the *Qiushu*, he invariably meant the new edition. Indeed, its revolutionary doctrine, Zhang's *raison d'être*, becomes clear only with this new *Qiushu*. However, Zhang was not just a revolutionary. To understand him as a figure in traditional Chinese intellectual history, we cannot ignore the old edition of the *Qiushu*.[34]

Aside from appendixes, the old edition of the *Qiushu* contains fifty essays, beginning with "Zun Xun" (Honor Xunzi) and ending with "Dusheng (xia)" (The sage alone, part 2). What we need to pay attention to here is the fact that the first six essays unmistakably constitute Zhang's study of the *zhuzi*. In other words, this book begins with a summary of the thought of the noncanonical thinkers of the pre-Qin era, who are drawn on and reorganized here as proponents of principles and ideas that might rescue China from her present situation of considerable difficulty.

First, Zhang praised Xunzi as the man who proposed basic ideals for the politics of his day. The essence of Xunzi's thought was to follow the model of the later kings, which implied the model of the kings of Xunzi's own day, as opposed to the earlier kings, namely the new, recent kings. The basis for this assertion is the idea that "the recent past is old [as in Old Text], while the distant past is new [as in New Text]." The *Spring and Autumn Annals* was written for a new king, and when Xunzi referred to the later kings, he meant an "uncrowned king." Following the model of the later kings thus meant following the *Spring and Autumn Annals*. However, while Zhang was elaborating this theory of a New Text bent, one can clearly see the Old Text aspect in which Zhang would, as always, argue that this was the position of Xunzi. Several years later Zhang would return once again to this subject. Kang Youwei, Liang Qichao, and others of the New Text school detested Xunzi the most. Kang and Liang had taken the basic position that Xunzi's emphasis on ritual was the first step in the distortion of the teachings of Confucius.

Zhang next moved to his second chapter, "Ru Mo" (Confucianism and Mohism), in which he expounded the greatness of Mozi. While pointing out how Confucians had misconstrued Mozi's notion of "universal love," he also noted that because of Mozi's principled "Opposition to Music" and "Short Funerals" [two names of chapters from the *Mozi*] he had lost the people's hearts. The principle of universal love, Zhang argued, was precisely the same as the main point made by Zhang Zai (Zhang Hengju, 1020–77) in his famous "Ximing" (Western inscription).

The third chapter of the *Qiushu*, entitled "Ru Dao" (Confucianism and Daoism), argued that the "pure and passive" (*qingjing*) stance taken by Laozi was wily and highly vindictive, and that it clearly opposed the principles of the Confucians who felt it shameful to "win the empire through the commission of a single act of unrighteousness or the execution of a single innocent person."[35] Zhang claimed that the Daoist principles of Laozi had provided the basis for politicians to do their work throughout the ages.

In his next chapter, "Ru Fa" (Confucianism and Legalism), Zhang argued that Legalists should absolutely never be absent from the political scene, and he vehemently defended Shang Yang (d. 338 B.C.E.) as the founder of Legalism. He also singled out the views of Guanzi (d. 645 B.C.E.), who used forms and names to put the state in good order. Citing the words attributed to Confucius's disciple Zhonggong (Ranyong)—"I can understand that such a man might do as a ruler, provided he were scrupulous in his own conduct and lax only in his dealings with the people"[36] —Zhang praised what might here be called a Confucian-Legalist sovereign. Throughout he used the expressions Confucian-Mohist, Confucian-Daoist, and Confucian-Legalist, indicating an effort on his part to find a new path for Chinese politics on the basis of a fusion of Mohism, Daoism, and Legalism with Confucianism. This concern is readily apparent in this chapter on Confucianism and Legalism.

In Chapter Five of the *Qiushu*, "Ru xia" (Confucianism and knights-errant), Zhang exhibited some rather distinctive traits. Since antiquity, he argued, the Confucians had spewed considerable venom in the direction of the knights-errant who originally were reviled by every one of the Hundred Schools and nine streams. Yet the highest deed a Confucian could execute was "to die in the performance of benevolence." Who was it, if not the knights-errant, who had eliminated great evils from the state and defended the state in times of great calamity? The reform movement of the late Qing did spawn a new trend toward respect for the knights-errant, but in the case of Zhang Binglin the importance with which he regarded them was a consequence solely of their having originally been one of the Hundred Schools and nine streams of thought. (Of course, the knights-errant were not among the "Hundred Schools and nine streams" of thought. In developing this point after 1911, in his *Jianlun*, Zhang went so far as to compare the famous Dao Zhi [a legendary bandit of high antiquity] with Bakunin.)[37]

Chapter Six, "Ru bing" (Confucianism and the military), is similar. It debates ideas about soldiers and the military, as well as military science, which were always held in low esteem by Confucians. This institution was not, he argued, to be looked down on, for the military had deep roots among the people, and this respect was continually encouraged by such ceremonies as the institution of local recommendation. Zhang claimed that the basis of a military should lie in controlling the spirit.

I have only introduced those chapters of the *Qiushu* that specifically discuss the *zhuzi*. Throughout the other forty or more chapters, Zhang offered his research and viewpoints concerning the *zhuzi* schools. Of course, there were quotations from European scholarship and thought as well as citations to Buddhist scripture, in accord with the atmosphere of the times. A Buddhist philosophy centering on Huayan and Weishi texts was a new idea at that time. Rather than analyze all the remaining sections of the *Qiushu*, I would like to look only at Chapter 29, entitled "Kedi."

The title "Kedi" is best translated as "guest emperor." This clearly implies that he was referring to the "Son of Heaven" after the Manchus had conquered China. As Zhang argued, military leaders and prominent taxation officials in contemporary China were *keqing* or "guest officials" (an expression originally employed in the Spring and Autumn and Warring States periods), all drawn from the ranks of Westerners. Thus, it was not in the least surprising that the Manchus had become "guest emperors," and reason dictated that "anti-Manchu ideas should be discarded" as useless. However, the "guest officials" were guests for whom there was a host, who made use of them. Who were the hosts in the case of the "guest emperors"? Zhang was restrained: "Stop! Don't say anything! Great music is lost on the ears of the villagers." He also laid bare his heart: "If someone commands us to speak, we shall say nothing. China's joint hosts [or common sovereigns, *gongzhu*], from the Han dynasty forward, have retained the same surname for over two thousand years. They are the descendants of Confucius." These common sovereigns of China lived continuously in the village known as Qufu; those revered as emperor for the previous two thousand years were Duke Huan of Qi and Duke Wen of Jin in the Zhou era, much like the Japanese *bakufu*.

For our present concerns, the point in the old edition of the *Qiushu* to which we need pay most attention is undoubtedly Zhang's assertion that Confucius and his family line were the common or joint sovereigns of China. It seems to me that the basis of this conception was less the relationship between kings and hegemons in the Zhou era than the Japanese emperor system, with its claim to a single family line of ten thousand generations. Be that as it may, in this period Zhang conceived of the disciples of Confucius, like Confucius himself, as the joint sovereigns of China. He could tolerate the presence of the emperors of the various and sundry dynasties through history only on the basis of the fiction that their status as emperor was sanctioned by the joint sovereigns. This notion of joint sovereigns, seen from the perspective of the family line of the founder of a religion, is not unconnected to Kang Youwei's notion of a religious founder.

The fiftieth and final chapter of the *Qiushu*, entitled "Dusheng (part 2)," argued that the reason Confucius alone qualified as the sage extraordinaire past and present was that he was the first to forge a pathway to a world of reason from the ancient world of magic and firmly establish the proper way of human relations; he then reorganized the classical texts, *Shijing* (Classic of poetry), *Shujing* (Classic of history), and the like, in which correct human relations were described, so as to transmit this message to subsequent generations. Zhang saw this conception of Confucius, as joint sovereign of China, to be the essence of the man.

The 1904 edition of the *Qiushu* contains the following entry as an opening page prior to the Table of Contents: "Correction of Errors in the Chapter 'Kedi.'" Here, Zhang renounced his own views of several years earlier, for, in the aftermath of the Boxer Uprising, he came to an explicitly revolutionary point of view. His earlier chapter "Kedi," as he now remarked in a statement of self-criticism, "was no more than reverence for a religious doctrine [*jiao*, as in *Kongjiao*, Confucian religion, or *jiaozhu*, religious founder, as opposed to *xue* or school of thought] that

adorned the inattentive mind and ignored the essence of things."
He went on to say that the patriotism of scholars and the ani-
mosity of the populace could not be realized unless the Manchus
were driven out. One country after another had invaded China,
ultimately turning her into the "double slave" (a slave of slaves)
of Europe and the United States. By way of censuring his own
earlier view for being incapable of advocating independence for
China and for seeking help from the spiritual legacy of Confucius, Zhang now expressly claimed to have rewritten the old text
of the *Qiushu* to expunge this view.

Zhang added to the new *Qiushu* a second chapter entitled
"Ding Kong" (Correcting Confucius). He argued here that the
appearance of Confucius in China truly marked the root of
China's tragedy. The fact that China had lost the spirit of enterprise and stood on the verge of demise today was not the fault or
crime of Confucius, but these problems originated when his
emergence was used to consolidate authority and conservatism.[38]
In his morality and scholarship, Confucius was inferior to both
Mencius and Xunzi, according to Zhang, and to honor Confucius for his learning and thought was just empty praise.

Yet, in Zhang's formulation, although Confucius may have
been inferior to Mencius and Xunzi in his morality and scholarship, one point had always to be kept firmly in mind: Confucius
was "a fine historian of antiquity." With the assistance of Zuo
Qiuming, Confucius had edited the *Spring and Autumn Annals*.
Compared to the *zhuzi*, one might call him the North Star. Sima
Tan (d. 110 B.C.E.) and Sima Qian (145?–86? B.C.E.) continued
this work, and subsequently the *Qilüe* [Seven Summaries, an ordering of all known writings into seven categories] appeared.
Following Confucius, the author of the *Qilüe*, Liu Xin of the Former Han dynasty, the very Liu Xin whom Kang Youwei had ac-
cused of being the criminal forger of the Confucian classics, was
for Zhang Binglin on a par in name and deed with Confucius.
The *Qilüe* was a work that began by classifying and ordering according to filiation the achievements of the *zhuzi* schools. It later
became the basis for the "Bibliographic Treatise" in the *Hanshu*.

In the July 1906 issue of *Guocui xuebao* (Journal of national essence), Zhang published his essay "Zhuzi xueshuo lüe" (Outlines of the theories of the *zhuzi*).[39] This may be considered in effect Zhang's final statement on the works of the *zhuzi*. As is often noted, it was the first work on the schools of thought of the *zhuzi* in the form of a "history of Chinese philosophy" (or the first history of Chinese philosophy as a study of the *zhuzi* schools), a genre that flourished in great splendor later in the Republican period. Ordinarily, Zhang is given credit for reviving contemporary studies of the *zhuzi*, but this is far too general a statement. A pioneering work in contemporary *zhuzi* studies was the New Text volume by Kang Youwei, *Kongzi gaizhi kao*. Roughly ten years later, if we ignore the *Qiushu*, this article by Zhang, an Old Text school study of the *zhuzi*, appeared.

Zhang argued that the weakness of Chinese scholarship as a whole lay in a lack of coherence and a fuzziness in differentiating boundaries. After Emperor Wu of the Han dynasty established Confucianism as the sole orthodox doctrine, no matter how much irresponsible or high-minded chatter was expended, one might offer an altogether farfetched notion so long as one did so without attacking Confucius. However, in the case of the *zhuzi* of the Zhou and Qin eras, each of them persisted in their own system of thought and walked their own independent paths, without making use of the others' work or supporting one another. Thus, Xunzi ruthlessly criticized, indeed denounced, Confucius's twelve disciples (Zisi and Mencius among them). This situation was clearly quite different from that of subsequent generations, who came to despise narrow-mindedness and to esteem tolerance, to hate the divisions set up to separate scholarly groups and to brag about their farsightedness.

There were, of course, criticisms of these developments, but one can locate here the origin of the difference between the learning that explicated the classics and that of the *zhuzi*. The "learning based on explaining the classics" was objective; it studied laws, institutions, facts; it did not discuss right and wrong or search for principles of proper behavior. The learning of the *zhuzi*, by contrast, was subjective; any book might be of use to one's school of thought, and there was no need in the least for partisan attacks.

What one had first to understand in order to do a study of the *zhuzi*, Zhang argued, was that "learning" (*xue*) in ancient times arose among the kings' officials (the officials of various professional specialties at court). There was no such thing as "learning" among the common people. If one considered engaging in scholarship, one had to become an official and to serve in a state office. Without official service, there was no learning, and vice versa; learning and service were one. Prime Minister Li Si (d. 208 B.C.E.) of the Qin dynasty once said that anyone who wished to study the law must take an official as his teacher. This example suggests that such was the way in ancient times. In the various offices of state, specialized scholarly work was transmitted for generations without contact with the scholarship of other offices. With the decline of central state offices in the Warring States period, these specialized scholarly enterprises began to flow out among the people, giving birth to the Hundred Schools of the *zhuzi*. Accordingly, the various *zhuzi*—Confucians, Daoists, Legalists, and the like—preserved their distinctive traditions without mixing.

Zhang Binglin's views on the origins of Chinese scholarship ultimately were based in the "Bibliographic Treatise" of the *Hanshu*, but more recently in the work of Zhang Xuecheng (1738–1801). In this period early in the twentieth century, the writings of Zhang Xuecheng had been rediscovered and re-evaluated, and they were common knowledge among Chinese intellectuals.[40]

The Confucians, Zhang continued, came originally from educational officials of the Zhou. As it said in the prime minister's section in the *Zhouli* [Rites of Zhou], "The Confucians (*Ru*) take as their way the winning over of the people." Their duty was to serve exclusively in education, which is to say they taught the people in three areas: the Six Virtues [wisdom, benevolence, sincerity, righteousness, moderation, and harmony], the Six Obligations of Conduct [filial piety, friendship, kindness, love of one's kin, endurance on behalf of others, and charity], and the

Six Arts [propriety, music, archery, charioteering, writing, and mathematics]. Thus, since Confucius was widely learned and multi-talented, the Confucians taught the way of sincerity and sympathy to others.

There were, however, two sides to Confucius: the man who had reordered history in his revision of the Six Classics;[41] and the man who engaged in education, as he appears in the *Analects* and the *Xiaojing* (Classic of filial piety). The first Confucius spawned a line of "teachers of the classics," while the second Confucius spawned a line of "Rujia" or Confucians. From the Han dynasty forward, the distinction between these two groups became less and less sharp, though the two should always be distinguished, Zhang argued. The former took the search for truth as their job, while the latter aimed at making learning useful. What the latter sought was ideal practice; the former, the determination of facts, learning for learning's sake. Teachers of the classics were often reviled as decadent scholars who were unfamiliar with events in the real world, but one should never forget the point that they were indifferent to wealth and fame. The defect in the Confucians, Zhang claimed, was their objective of wealth and fame.

Furthermore, they never dared try to become sovereign themselves. Great Confucians were content simply to assist their sovereign, while lesser Confucians merely sought to become Grand Masters (*dafu*) and Servicemen (*shi*) [second and third rank officials, respectively, in the Zhou] to their feudal lord. Setting one's mind on doing something was considered vulgar. Confucius had said [in response to Zigong's query about what to do with a beautiful gem]: "Sell it! Sell it!"[42] This, too, was a frank expression of the principle of seeking wealth and renown. Robber Zhi [a figure for whom a chapter in the *Zhuangzi* is named] had derisive things to say of Confucius, which point to the same conclusion:

This must be none other than that crafty hypocrite Kong Qiu [Confucius] from the state of Lu! . . . You eat without ever plowing, clothe yourself without ever weaving. Wagging your lips, clacking your tongue, you invent any kind of "right" or "wrong" that suits you, leading the rulers of the world away from the Source, capaciously setting up ideals of "filial piety" and "brotherliness," all the time trying to worm your way into favor with the lords of the fiefs or the rich and eminent![43]

Confucius's efforts to serve 72 lords constituted the beginning of the *youshuo* or itinerant philosophizers (originally this expression has a sordid or vulgar sense to it). Later, Confucians generally also became adherents of the idea of forging alliances between competing fiefs during the Warring States period. Confucius himself had argued that "[As for me I am different from any of these.] I have no 'thou shalt' or 'thou shalt not' ";[44] and "To be the gentleman means doing things at the appropriate time and place."[45] Mencius said of Confucius that, among the sages, "he was the most timely one."[46] Thus, the particular quality of Confucius's teachings was the fact that they "followed the trends of the times."

The implementation of righteousness also changed with the trends of the times. Hence, Confucius said [in response to a query from Zigong about men two ranks beneath those qualified to be "officers"]: "He who stands by his word . . . undertakes nothing that he does not bring to achievement."[47] The "Golden Mean" lay precisely with these *xiangyuan* or "villagers" [mentioned in the *Analects*]. Yet, Confucius berated such people: "The honest villagers spoil true virtue."[48] In fact, though, we should note that *xiangyuan* was a name used for people who lived in obscurity in villages and disregarded local officials.

Those who controlled a large stretch of territory, wore a broad imperial gown, and in their words and deeds embellished the surface with falsity, and in so doing deluded the sovereign of the realm, these men should be called *guoyuan* [i.e., the national-level counterpart of the *xiangyuan*], according to Zhang. They were far worse, Zhang claimed, than the *xiangyuan*. Confucius may have disparaged the *xiangyuan*, but not so the *guoyuan*. People should know of the latter's greed. To the extent that they drew on Confucian morality, they were merely competing for monetary gain. There was not a single instance, it seemed, when they acted with rage and energy in the face of difficulties. As the old saying had it: "Don't buy good land to enrich your family; there are countless kinds of grain in books."[49]

This was an abuse Confucians were unable to avoid. Insofar as they employed Confucian ideals, they were wont not to explain principles clearly and in discussing them to remain highly vague and stale. The harm wrought by reverence for Christianity or Islam lay in their obstruction to men's thinking, but the harm wrought by Confucians lay in the confusion it brought to men's minds. This was the reason the Cheng brothers (Cheng Yi [1033–1107] and Cheng Hao [1032–85]), Zhu Xi, Lu Xiangshan (1139–92), and Wang Yangming all had authority but no substance.

Nonetheless, was Confucius completely without any merit? Zhang's answer was No. Confucius had thoroughly transformed a world of magic and mystery and worked hard in the affairs of men; he had also transformed the specialized, bureaucratic nature of learning and spread it to the common people. This achievement was genuinely unique throughout the ages. However, two thousand years had passed since his time, and all that now remained, in Zhang's estimation, was the zeal for wealth.

Zhang's essay "Outlines of the Theories of the *zhuzi*" described from his own distinctive point of view the Daoists, the Mohists, the Divinationists, the itinerant political theoreticians, the Legalists, the Logicians, the Agriculturalists, and others listed as the nine streams and Hundred Schools in the "Bibliographic Treatise" of the *Hanshu*. Missing throughout this essay was the view found in the *Qiushu* that in effect counted the "knights-errant" as one school among the *zhuzi*. In any event, as a late-Qing introduction to the schools of the *zhuzi*, Zhang's essay is the equal of Kang Youwei's *Kongzi gaizhi kao*.

Contrary to what was undoubtedly the most widely held view of Confucius among Confucians at the time—Confucius as an educator, the "model teacher for ten thousand generations"—Zhang fixed on the thesis of Confucius the historian and father of learning. By clearly delineating the filiations of textual scholarship in the Qing era in which he himself was a participant, Zhang ferociously attacked the lineage of views associated with the former image of Confucius. That is, he attacked the views of those associated with the New Text school.

In his well-known article of 1913, "Bo Kang Youwei lun geming shu" (Letter attacking Kang Youwei's views on revolution), Zhang had already noted that Kang's principle of protecting the emperor was in fact nothing other than an ardent desire for wealth and fame. The Confucius that emerged from the *Qiushu* was a "fine historian," and this view is expanded and amplified militantly in "Outlines of the Theories of the *zhuzi*." It was a major conclusion derived from partisan principles that derived from Zhang's revolutionary and scholarly views. He was becoming aware in an ever more definitive manner that his own views, inspired by the *Zuozhuan*, stood opposed to those of the *Gongyang Commentary*, and that his Old Text association clearly stood in opposition to the New Text school.

At the outset we noted the emergence of the image of Confucius as a *zhuzi*, a conclusion ultimately reached by Qing *kaozhengxue*. Among the views of Confucius as a *zhuzi*, however, the now nationalist revolutionary Zhang Binglin established the image of Confucius as a historian as well as the father of learning; and this stance was firmly opposed to the image of Confucius as a "religious founder" that had emerged earlier. Several things played undeniably major roles in Zhang's coming to this thesis on Confucius, a view he seems to have approached while in Japan: the Western idea of knowledge for its own sake, an idea easily accommodated in *kaozhengxue* of the Qing period; the recognition that every ethnic group or nationality had its own distinctive form of knowledge and intellectual tradition; and the recognition that the three indices that defined the individuality of a cultural tradition were geographic environment, political practices, and ethnic character.

Although adopting a revolutionary stance, Zhang could hardly deny the utilitarian [aspect of Kang Youwei's position]. Yet by strictly differentiating knowledge from action—that is, by coming out boldly in a critique of *kaozhengxue* for "separating the classics from the Way"—he gave his ethnic nationalism more vividness. Gu Yanwu (1613–82), whom Kang Youwei from his ardently reformist position had attacked as the man responsible for the decline of learning, was now transformed by Zhang and reaffirmed as a great teacher in the Chinese scholarly tradition, a man worthy of admiration and respect. The reason for this transformation was that the basis of nationalism lay not in theories, but in a genuine love of the ethnic group. Only by accurately examining and chronicling the past of one's ethnic group, good and bad, beautiful and ugly alike, could one arrive at such a love.[50]

There is room for considerable doubt whether the view of Confucius and Confucianism elaborated by Zhang was shared by the revolutionaries of the 1911 period. In any event, though, one must truly recognize that this new perspective on Confucius and Confucianism emerged from the views of the nationalistic revolutionaries in their fierce debate with the reformers. For Zhang this debate simultaneously entailed the struggle of the Old Text school against the New Text school. In the Republican period, this perspective—a fundamental awareness of "national learning" or national heritage—broadly permeated the scholarly world, together with the awareness of the need to "reorganize the national heritage" (*guogu zhengli*), which had originated with Kang Youwei.

The final description by Zhang of this view of Confucius was not published until after the 1911 Revolution; although it appeared in December 1913, I would like to introduce his "Bo Kongjiao jianli yi" (Refutation of the petition to establish a Confucian religion).[51] This essay constituted Zhang's manifesto of opposition to Kang Youwei's ideas for a Confucian religion, which came pouring forth shortly after the establishment of the Republic of China, and to the movement for Confucian churches organized under Kang's influence. Kang's representative writings on behalf of a Confucian religion have been translated in full [into Japanese]; to redress the balance, what follows is a complete translation of this 1913 essay by Zhang Binglin.

Refutation of the Petition to Establish a Confucian Religion

Recently men have been advocating the establishment of Confucian churches, and I for one have to deplore this bizarre inanity. Being something extremely inferior, religion was popular among the common folk in the earliest days of antiquity. That it did not die out thereafter was simply because it was difficult for men to act contrary to custom. It was assuredly not because men revered it and were loath to part with it.

Originally, China had no national religion. Because the promulgation of the five religions by Shun and the announcement of the twelve religions in the Zhou fell under the jurisdiction of a bureaucrat known as the *situ* or Minister of Education, these "religions" were not studied in the schools. Hence, they were authoritative teachings, comparable to what we today would call social education and not something that would fit into the category of religion.

Where the *Yijing* (Classic of change) says that the "sage establishes his teachings in accordance with the Way of Heaven," this is just like the same text's line about "not encouraging the washing of the hands."[52] In the matter of the "great sacrifice," Confucius said that he "did not know" what it meant.[53] Thus, although he said he would "establish his teachings," Confucius in fact did not do so.

When one looks at the officials who served the gods in the *Rites of Zhou*, all were under the control of the king's officials; they were not at work among the general populace. When the Zhou was in decline, both Confucius and Laozi were well-known personalities in the world. Laozi said: "[Ruling a big state is like cooking a small fish.] If you rule the realm with the Way [of nonaction], spirits will not affect you, nor will your soul know weariness."[54] Confucius did not speak of deities, nor did he work for the soul. Followers of these two men—Zhuangzi, Mencius, Xunzi, Gongsun Long, Shen Buhai, Hanfeizi, and others—all appeared around the same time. They constructed analytic logics and examined phenomena in the human realm. As a result, magic spells came to an end, and the people were revived.

About two thousand years ago, Buddhism entered China from a foreign land, and following that the Yellow Turbans [a Daoist-inspired group of rebels at the end of the Later Han dynasty] arose. There were elements in each of these cases that looked like religion. Originally, however, Buddhism did not revere deities;

it was fundamentally concerned with fixed contemplation and perfect wisdom and its exquisite theories were finely detailed. Occasionally, though, some strange ideas arising in India entered the mix coming to China; yet China's great scholars did not focus their attention on such things. Furthermore, Buddhists would not marry, ate simple vegetation, and wore rough woolen clothing, and their behavior approached that of recluses. Such men could never be teachers of the general populace.

The Daoist priests of the Yellow Turbans misled the people with their nonsense about talismans and amulets and their heretical ideas. Scholars who understood all this had no desire whatsoever to get near it. Thus, while Buddhism was not a religion, the Yellow Turbans were no different from those practitioners of the *Classic of Change* who were ridiculed by the people or from fortune-tellers. In other words, China did not yet at that time have religion.

That was the whole story. There were mysterious [ostensibly religious] elements in the historical traces left by [figures from China's legendary antiquity] such as Fuxi and the Yellow Emperor, but later generations have honored such figures only for [their inventions of] agriculture, fishing, and clothing. As persistent characteristics of the Chinese people, one should note their attentiveness to political matters and to daily life; they work hard at commerce and farming; their minds are set solely on the scope of life here and now; and they do not try to discuss anything that goes beyond their experiences.

The people esteem self-respect and have no desire to turn the spirits into deities, nor do they wish to gamble with their lives in serving a particular spirit. This is the very reason for the great insight of the ancient Chinese (*Hua-Xia*) people. The difference between wisdom and foolishness is great indeed when one compares this to those who curry favor with their God or pay respects to their Pope, their entire nation serving a single authority specified in its constitution.[55]

If one were dying of an illness and prayed to a spiritual medium, should prayer prove inefficacious, one would immediately turn one's back and switch one's prayers to ten other deities or spirits. Take, for example, someone who spreads out many nets and waits for pheasants and hares. He is trying his hand at catching the game; there is no particularly firm religious belief at work here. The rational person approaches [religion] with an attitude of indifference; the fool approaches half-believing and half-doubting with an attitude that he will not use it but will not throw it out either. In short, the Chinese people, seen as a whole, do not look up to a single religion.

Seeing how the teachings of Jesus and Martin Luther gradually spread to our country, they are trying to resist it by establishing a "Confucian religion." Is this not just like causing a burn in order to create a scar even though there was originally no injury? They are vainly copying a vulgar phenomenon that will have no utility whatsoever for China.

On the special *shangding* day [of the second and eighth months of the lunar calendar] in antiquity, the festival for Confucius merely entailed the offering of aromatic grasses. In the Tang dynasty, [Prime Minister] Li Linfu (d. 752) ordered that throughout the land there should be offerings of sacrificial oxen, and [the poet] Liu Yuxi (772–842) ridiculed this as ignorant. Thereafter, the Confucian temples became just like the institutions of the imperial family, imitating the main imperial palaces in form and with special instrumental music prepared [as with the Emperor's special orchestra]. Nonetheless, the temple halls were housed temporarily within schools, and only Confucian scholars made pilgrimages there. The officials in charge performed ceremonies only at the prescribed times, and they never carried them out before society at large.

In other words, Confucius was the honored object of students [who were given quasi-official privileges in law]. This is just like carpenters who honor [as a guardian deity] Gongshuzi [also known as Gongshu Ban], tailors who honor Xuanyuan [another name for the Yellow Emperor], or bureaucrats who honor Xiao He.[56] They revere the progenitors of their professions and earnestly seek their roots. In no sense whatsoever are they serving them as deities or spirits; the existence of the soul or spirit of the objects of their reverence is never raised as an issue, nor is this a widespread phenomenon among the people.

In the beginning clothing and homes were necessities in the

lives of the populace; laws and documents [handled by bureaucrats] could not be destroyed in a day by the government. If this was because the people prayed to Confucius and considered him the founder of a religion, then surely the Yellow Emperor, Gongshuzi, and Xiao He would all be founders of religions as well. Life's necessities change over time, making contemporary institutions different from those of antiquity, and these three gentlemen thus have no value as religious names. This being the case, the institutions of the Republic [of China], which we have just created, certainly differ from those of the Spring and Autumn period; the customs of the populace have no use for scholarly rituals. The regulations concerning the *qicui* and *zhancui* mourning garb are being abolished along with the crime of incest.

How in the world can Confucius be called the founder of a religion today? While violating the basic principle [for qualifying as the founder of a religion], seeking to make his image alone the object of reverence is tantamount to a display of mendacity. To stress only one school and forget about other, similar ones is biased. No matter how you approach it, it is baseless. To cling to superstition and try to imitate a religion with it clearly must not be a law of the universe.

When you think about it, in the late Zhou era Confucius was just on a par with Bo Yi and Liuxia Hui.[57] Both Mencius and Xunzi praised him from the bottom of their hearts; but, when it came to a great man for all generations or a moral hero, they saw him as evenly matched by Yao, Shun, King Wen, and King Wu. Never did they think of him as one deserving the rites befitting Heaven or an imperial ancestor. Yet, Daoist alchemists of [the states of] Yan and Qi [in the Han dynasty] spread to the Donghai region [along the coast of Shandong and Jiangsu provinces], and those who expounded the classics often mixed in elements of sorcery. For example, although the "Hongfan" (The great plan [a chapter in the *Classic of History*]) was just a document among the ancient writings, [these Daoists] jokingly extended their discussions and forced all sorts of ideas into it.

The originator of this sort of behavior was Fu Sheng (fl. 2d century B.C.E.), and the man who expanded the practice widely was Dong Zhongshu (179?–104? B.C.E.). In the era when the group of [Daoist alchemists of the Han dynasty] Shaojun, Wencheng, and Wuli were appointed to posts, Dong Zhongshu was predicting fires, and he vied with them over such things as deliverance from droughts and stopping rainfall. He regarded the classical texts as if they were the prognostications of a sorcerer; and, on this basis, he added his own twists to the text of the *Spring and Autumn Annals*. He argued that the *Spring and Autumn Annals* was a work that established [Kang Youwei said "reformed"] institutions for the Han dynasty. In so doing, Dong flattered the sovereign of the day and threw politics into disorder. The asinine emperor then [Wu] was unable to see through all this, and he was convinced that Confucius was actually the son of the Black Emperor and was truly a Daoist immortal.

Prophecies appeared all at once, and bizarre theories began to spread in public. Dong Zhongshu was a harbinger of the sudden eruption [in 91 B.C.E.] of a palace rebellion under Emperor Wu, which was based on superstitious beliefs. Thereafter, when a natural calamity occurred, a prime minister would be punished with death and collateral relatives of the emperor would be extinguished. In the process, sorcery wrought havoc with the institutions of the land, and matters of the spirits violated politics. Throughout the Han era, political affairs were always accompanied by religious matters.

Initially, Dong Zhongshu claimed for Confucius precisely what Gong Chong [a mystic from Shandong during the reign of Emperor Xun, r. 126–45, of the Later Han] and Zhang Daoling [a mountain hermit of the Later Han] did for Laozi. Those who today are calling for a Confucian religion are merely copying the model set by Dong Zhongshu.[58] They claim that Confucius has been honored generation after generation without change, and that if this ceased today, the pathway for humanity would be cut off, and the basic principles of politics and society would probably be destroyed. They seem to understand only that we must revere Confucius, but they have no idea why. I would like to raise the following points in order to respond to people's expectations. The reason Confucius is the Big Dipper of China lies in the facts that he created history, he disseminated written texts, he promoted scholarship, and he eliminated differences in status between men.

The *Classic of History* was a text covering a long stretch of time in bits and pieces, and it recorded events as they occurred. It was very difficult to comprehend the factual details with clarity. But once Confucius had prepared the *Spring and Autumn Annals*, a proper chronicle came into being and the factual details became clearer and clearer. Thereafter, Zuo Qiuming wrote a commentary on the *Spring and Autumn Annals*, and Sima Qian and Ban Gu (32–92) continued in this [historical] vein. In their work "history" reached radiant perfection. Their examples became models passed on to subsequent generations. Later eras were able to understand antiquity, and later men could understand men of former times. Thus, although barbarians invaded and our national destiny was on the brink of collapse, the people were able to forge an attachment to their past and suddenly rise in rebellion. This point is the first contribution that Confucius made to the Chinese people.

The curriculum ordained for local schools in the *Rites of Zhou* was limited to the Six Arts. Yet, the Great Ceremony "was not to be passed down to the common people" [even though *li* or propriety was one of the Six Arts]. At that time, the preservation of works concerning the political systems of the sage kings was under the control of the court's Keeper of Temple Treasures (*tianfu*). The political materials [contained therein] were virtually all recorded in the *Classic of Poetry* and the *Classic of History*. The Palace Master (*shishi*) instructed the pupils in the National University, although the general populace was excluded from this institution. Even if the common people wanted to learn about antiquity, they had no means of receiving instruction. Thus, it is written in the ancient texts: "They studied how to be officials, and they served the Regional Mentor (*shi*)"; and "They studied with the Grand Master (*dafu*)."[59] If one were unable to become a servant to a high official, one had no way to learn anything about antiquity. Confucius said: "Read the books in the Zhou imperial library." With the attitude of a "transmitter, not a creator,"[60] Confucius had collected the Six Classics together and disseminated them among the people; only then did the general populace come to understand norms. Every home became familiar with the classical texts. This was his second great achievement.

Originally, each of the Hundred Schools and nine streams of thought derived from official offices. Each of the *zhuzi* preserved only his own school of thought and did not read widely in the texts [of other areas of knowledge]. Thus, it was impossible for learning to cohere. Confucius caused the written texts to spread, composed his own commentary to the *Classic of Change*, delivered himself of the words of the *Analects*, and invested profound thoughts within it. Great teachers and famous Confucians appeared one after the next, who, although they expressed their own opinions, similarly encouraged scholarship. This was Confucius's third great achievement.

Prior to the Spring and Autumn period, many bureaucratic positions were hereditary. Occasionally there were fishermen or shepherds who happened to encounter a sovereign and whose position in the world would rise, but this was not an ordinary event. It is not that there were never any brilliant minds among the general populace; they just could not gain intimacy with political writings. When it came to far-reaching policy, they were likely to be a hindrance and were in no position to oppose the hereditary officialdom.

Those who on rare occasions were appointed to posts were generally officials with a particular talent or merely a scribe. Yet, Confucius spread the written texts, trained three thousand disciples, traveled with them to 72 states, distinguished the different kinds of peoples, gained a complete knowledge of regional qualities and products, and came to learn about the governments of the various states. His disciples and followers sought to become salaried officials and contested the views of rulers. Within one hundred years of the death of Confucius, the Six States arose and hereditary officials went into decline. If people were able to gain even a little taste of learning, anyone might obtain a ministerial post. Thus, status differences disappeared, and the lower classes began to creep upward. Such a situation continues to the present day. This was Confucius's fourth great achievement.

If we can sum up these four achievements, Confucius was a pillar who protected the people and caused civilization to flourish. He was not the founder of a religion. Had a man we have come to know as Confucius not appeared in the world, political standards would not have been transmitted, scholarship would not have flourished, the state would have been destroyed by barbarians and never revived, and the people once fallen into degradation would not have been able to rise up. It would have been impossible for his name to rank among the civilized countries of the world. It is indeed because of this former sage that we have not yet perished. For this reason, Confucius ranks far higher than Yao, Shun, King Wen, or King Wu.

As for the teachings of morality, good behavior, benevolence, and righteousness, these the Zhou government was already implementing among the common people, and the various states of the time never compelled the destruction of the basic principles of political and social morality. As a result, there were sages such as Qu Yuan [343–277? B.C.E.; a model of a loyal minister, he committed suicide when his advice was not heeded] and Shi Qiu [fl. 534–493 B.C.E.; a model of the sagacious minister who pointed out evil where he saw it, a Grand Master of the state of Wei in the Spring and Autumn period], and beneath them men of morality such as Chang Ju and Jie Ni [contemporaries of Confucius who lived in seclusion away from the chaos of the world], or any of the eremitic figures of that time, who as men of morality spread their moral teachings over the earth without sternly lecturing people.

Of course, we cannot say that Confucius imparted everything [concerning morality, good behavior, benevolence, and righteousness]. Furthermore, Confucius's written works occasionally describe ceremonial events, where they came up in his editing of the ancient chronicles, but Confucius never affirmed such nonsensical things as Heaven or ghosts. This does not mean that he looked down on society, nor that he sought to frighten the common people. He did not want to expend the time and trouble to eliminate such things altogether. In this he was just like modern European philosophers who assume a vague attitude toward religion. Morality was not Confucius's monopoly; religion was something Confucius rejected. One would have to say, though, that those who forget what is to be revered in Confucius and what is not to be revered and then proceed to want to pray to him, these men actually do harm to Confucius and sully his great authority.

A discussant might respond that the reason to advocate a Confucian religion is to pacify Buddhist believers and to keep Mongolia and Tibet [Buddhist states] from harboring any ideas of revolt.[61] But, this is a deception pure and simple. Contrariness in Mongolia or Tibet would merely serve to provoke an estrangement on the pretext that powerful neighbors [namely, Russia and England] want China to abandon religion. In fact, religion is not the sort of thing that can be used to calm people down. In the past, when Zhang Juzheng (1525–82) brought Mongolia under control, he both attacked them militarily and won over their hearts and minds. Military force and political power are both necessary. Only after an overall allegiance had been established did he merely firm it up with the Lamaist religion. Now, though, they are not about to make military preparations, but are just using lies to try and forge links. It is like the story of reading the *Classic of Filial Piety* to the Yellow Turban bandits in an effort to make them surrender.[62] There is no reason that it should work. If they attempt to conciliate others with Buddhism, there is no reason why they should take part in the destruction of temples.[63] What is more, you cannot cajole people by thoughtlessly manufacturing some "Confucian religion."

Because the "Confucian religion" is not something that has long existed, it is not now a subject to be discarded. If it is not something to be abolished, then it is not something that can be constructed [anew]. In my view, carrying out a ceremony [of respect for Confucius] in the schools is perfectly appropriate, but to establish this as a religion impedes reason's road to progress and is a source of discord in the great way to peace. It must be regarded as an action lacking in moderation.

* * *

The foregoing is a complete translation of Zhang Binglin's argument against a Confucian religion. He raised three main points laid down by Kang Youwei and the reformist, New Text (Gongyang) school: Confucius was recognized as one of the *zhuzi*; there was a religious, mysterious quality to Confucius's birth, and he was the founder of a religion based on reform; and, furthermore, the content of his teachings was entirely unmysterious, enlightened, and internationalist. By contrast, Zhang argued the position of the nationalist revolutionary, Old Text (Zuozhuan) school: he agreed that Confucius was one of the *zhuzi*; but maintained that in no way was Confucius a religious figure, but rather a historian and thus the benefactor of Chinese civilization; and, the content of his teachings was certainly rational. But, Zhang was not the least bit concerned with whether Confucius's views were enlightened, and the ideas that Confucius was peerless in the world and that a religion surrounding him should permeate the globe were, in his estimation, nothing but vapid exaggerations.

At the root of the positions taken by Kang and Zhang lay a difference in evaluation of religion itself (at whose core, to a greater or lesser extent, lay the mystery necessitated by religious faith) and, accompanying it, a firm belief in the essence of what made China significant with respect to the so-called "civilized" countries of Europe. Furthermore, there was a political battle going on here between reform and revolution, and, at the root of this conflict, one must not overlook the major role played by the struggle between cliques from traditional Chinese scholarship, New Text versus Old Text. Later, during the Republican period, Zhang made his opposition to a Confucian religion thoroughgoing, while simultaneously becoming, it should be noted, an ardent advocate of the "recite the classics" movement, a program calling for the Confucian classics to be made part of the regular curriculum in the school system.

Wu Yu (1872–1949), to whom we shall shortly turn, once remarked that Zhang's opposition to a Confucian religion and frank criticism of Confucianism became one of the sources of anti-Confucianism in the New Culture Movement during the May Fourth period.[64] Nonetheless, Zhang Binglin would himself eventually regret "those crazy, deceptive views I held over ten years ago when I recklessly doubted the wisdom of the sage." And he withdrew his earlier, totalistic critique of Confucius.[65]

The Qing Government's Policy on Confucius

We have thus far summarized views of Confucius that emerged in the revolutionary upsurge at the end of the Qing dynasty, on the eve of the 1911 Revolution, and then just after it. The most distinctive view of Confucius was that of Zhang Binglin, but one cannot say that this was a new perspective on Confucius predominant among the revolutionaries. "Most of the revolutionaries drank from the same stream as the reformers and differed from the reformers only in their aim of overthrowing the Manchu dynasty."[66] This generally held position contains one aspect of the truth. In any event, ultimately the position that sought the absolute negation of the authority of Confucius was at this point raised by neither the revolutionaries nor the reformers. Thus, insofar as it concerned Confucius, the Qing regime did not have a view fundamentally opposed to their activities to strike out at. Of course, it may have been difficult to propose endeavors such as the new dating system based on Confucius's birth (the revolutionaries wanted to use the birth of the Yellow Emperor), which seemed to deny the Qing dynasty's calendar. Aside from this, though, efforts such as Kang Youwei's plans for institutional reform with a Confucian religion might have been implemented without serious difficulty. Yet these reforms were all aborted with the failure of the Hundred Days Reform Movement of 1898.

A certain change can be detected at this time in the Qing government's treatment of Confucius. The view of Confucius held by scholars and intellectuals within the establishment remained what it had been in the past, and to an extent they assumed a position of trying to adapt to the times by portraying a highly enlightened Confucius. Such a picture of Confucius and Confucianism can be gained through a reading of the 1898 work by Zhang Zhidong (1837–1909), *Quanxue pian* (An exhortation to learning).

Rather more worthy of note, though, were the efforts encouraged by the Qing government to clarify positively and boost the position of Confucius in educational and ceremonial institutions. The "Imperial Regulations on Schools" of January 1904 were famous for enacting a system of modern schools, primarily in imitation of those in Japan.[67] Details of these rules can be found under the heading, "By stressing learning the classics well, middle and elementary schools should find a place for the teachings of the sage." It read as follows: "In foreign schools there is one religion. The Chinese classics constitute China's religion. If we fail to study the classics in school, then the Way of Yao, Shun, Yu, Tang, Kings Wen and Wu, the Duke of Zhou, and Confucius, as well as 'the three bonds and five constant relationships' will be completely abandoned, and China will probably not be able to build a strong state." Thus, in the elementary schools, from the first through the fifth grades, twelve of the thirty hours of classes each week were devoted to practicing and reading the classics. This was the nature of the curriculum that was enacted.

In addition, a wooden altar to Confucius was placed in the classrooms, and daily prayers to it were carried out. School principals and teachers stopped all classes to lead the students in prayer on the first and fifteenth of each month; and on the two days of the Spring and Autumn Sacrifices to Confucius and his birthday on the 27th day of the eighth month of the old lunar calendar, they performed the three kneelings and nine knockings [i.e., the kowtow] together. Such occasions provided opportunities for school principals to lecture on the "Main points of revering Confucius and loving and respecting the great Qing state." Following the promulgation of the "Imperial Regulations on Schools," along with the altars for Confucius there were placed in each classroom tablets reading "Long live the Empress Dowager" and "Long live the Emperor!"

With the establishment two years later, in 1906, of the Ministry of Education, a modern, central agency for the administration of education, the government promulgated "Imperial Educational Guidelines" to elucidate the basic direction of education in the new schools.[68] These "Guidelines" contained five items: "There are two principles that will reject alien doctrines by immediately clarifying that which is intrinsic to Chinese education; these are loyalty to one's sovereign and reverence for Confucius. There are three principles to be encouraged in rapidly probing that which is most lacking in the character of the Chinese people; these are honoring the public, honoring the martial spirit, and honoring authenticity." Then, an explanation is affixed for each of these five points. For example, under the rubric "loyalty to one's sovereign," the "Guidelines" note that the Japanese educational system most emphasized Japan's unbroken imperial line and that the profound benevolence of the Qing dynasty had lasted several hundred years.

With respect to "reverence for Confucius," the text claims that it has been a grave error to belittle the teachings of the sages and reject ethical obligations since the arrival in China of Western theories. If we might summarize this item, education in all countries must emphasize and protect in full each country's spoken and written languages, history, customs, and religion. Thus, there would be a room in each of the schools to honor the national religion. The Way of Confucius, these "Guidelines" continued (and I paraphrase), was enormously expansive; not only was it unchanging for countless generations in China, but Confucius was a sage who was also esteemed by all the peoples of the world. It was said that the Japanese movement to revere the Emperor and overthrow the *bakufu* [culminating in the Meiji Restoration of 1868] was an accomplishment of Chinese learning. The learning and technical ability of the Japanese people has come in recent years to stand shoulder to shoulder with that of the West. They have inculcated their students with the brilliant words of our sages and burnished their spirit by stirring them to fidelity and righteousness. Indeed, Confucius was born in China, and he has been revered through the ages. In all schools large and small, classical learning will become a mandatory part of the curriculum; we must compose hymns of praise for Confucius to transform this "modern" decadence. On the Spring and Autumn sacrifices for Confucius and on his birthday, music must be played and ceremonies performed in all the schools.

There is one further point that needs to be noted. In the past only the middle-level sacrifices were performed in the Confucian temples, and these were now elevated in status to national sacrifices.[69] The Ministry of Education requested this change in a memorial of December 1907, a summary of which follows.

An edict was previously issued in which the "Guidelines" for education were laid down. It clearly stated five points—loyalty to one's sovereign, reverence for Confucius, honoring the public, honoring the martial spirit, and honoring authenticity—but the essence of it was reverence for Confucius. Today, the pollution of foreign customs has become severe, and our defense of the Way must be ever more strict. When a Western sovereign succeeds to the throne, he immediately proclaims an oath of religious faith to the effect that wherever his people shall go, there too he will send missionaries and there too he will build churches. Presumably, he is giving religion a priority; and, by setting it first, even if it undergoes countless changes, ensuring that it will not veer from its foundations.

In China, though, Confucius seems to occupy a secondary position, and only middle-level sacrifices are performed in Confucian temples. It is hoped that an enhancement of the national sacrifices will be proclaimed by our sovereign. If this memorial is approved, ceremonies at the Confucian temples will be like ceremonies of Heaven and Earth and those at the imperial temple of the Qing court [i.e., national rites]. The emperor will attend them personally.

I have spoken of various institutions involved in education and the elevation in status of the sacrifices to Confucius to a national level. With regard to the actual implementation of these plans, I have often also touched on the comparison with Christianity in the West. For the Qing court, which had branded Kang Youwei a traitor and absolutely forbade his stepping on Chinese soil, one might even argue that to a certain extent this amounted to a gradual implementation of Kang's ideals.

The Socialists and Anarchists: Sprouts of Confucius Rejected

At the time of the 1911 Revolution, one revolutionary wing comprised a fair number of men and women who had already taken the baptismal waters of socialism or anarchism and been transformed into a new form of revolutionary. In Tokyo there was a group surrounding Liu Shipei (1884–1919), Zhang Ji (1882–1947), and others; and in Paris there was a group surrounding Wu Zhihui (1865–1953) and Li Shizeng (1881–1973), among others. Both groups are better considered anarchists than socialists. The Tokyo group published the organ *Tianyi* (Natural justice), while the Paris group published their organ *Xin shiji* (New century). These two journals took extraordinarily radical positions in their rejection of Confucianism. However, not a single one of their articles identified Confucius in particular as the object of any concentrated attack.

In her article, "Nüzi fuqiu lun" (On women's revenge, published in *Xin shiji*), He Zhen (the wife of Liu Shipei) listed cases of the oppression of women by men throughout history and denounced them all. "What they call etiquette is in fact just a disgrace. What they call the principle of righteousness is in fact just shamelessness. . . . If we don't wipe away all the wicked doctrines of Confucianism, we shall have no hope for [future] glory."[70]

In 1907 *Xin shiji* carried an article entitled "Sangang geming" (Revolution in the three constant relationships).[71] Taking a position based on the "scientific truth" of equality, the article rejected the "three constant relationships," namely those between sovereign and subject, father and son, and husband and wife. Strangely, there is not a single mention of either Confucius or Confucianism anywhere in this piece. In only one essay in any issue of *Xin shiji* (in 1908) was Confucius mentioned by name and attacked.[72] This was a contribution entitled "Fei Kong weiyan" (Abolish Confucius's subtle words), and it is signed "Jue sheng"

(Eliminate the sage). This piece corresponds to what we would expect. It reads in part as follows:

Fear and superstition are the bases of power. Religions reinforce superstition with fear, and governments use superstition to reinforce fear. A religious revolution is difficult, but political revolution is easy. A political revolution in a country where politics and religion are entwined is difficult. The rise and fall, prosperity or decline, of a single race moves in proportion to the depth of its superstition. Contemporary commentators take an erroneous position that ignores science when they claim in a haphazard fashion that Western civilization owes its success to its Protestantism. The very fact that Western civilization exists today is due solely to the strength of scientific discovery. We must not neglect for even a single day a revolution in superstition.

China is a country in which politics and religion are entwined. It is a country of fear and superstition. Nowadays, it is just dreaming nonsense to talk of such things as a constitution. The one who caused such calamities is none other than Confucius. I won't raise the issue of whether Confucius was a religious figure or not. But, from considering the facts that the government made use of him and the people are superstitious, if this is not a religious phenomenon, there is no way to explain it.

Well then, Confucius provided the foundations for autocratic government and bitterly poisoned our fellow countrymen for over two thousand years. Now, once again, our fellow countrymen adhere in awe to the spirits of ancestral tablets when carrying out ritual ceremonies. Let us put aside the exultations of the Constitutionalist Party. It is incredibly bizarre that the enthusiastic advocates of revolution are either praising the *zhuzi* of the Zhou and Qin periods or castigating men of the Song and Yuan [the Zhu Xi school], but no one has turned his attention to Confucius himself. If the ancestral tablet of national sacrifice isn't dumped into a temple fire, the political revolution will make no gains at all. Furthermore, why do we raise questions about a gender revolution? Why do we raise questions about an anarchist revolution? It is said that if you want to capture thieves, you should first go after their leader. Isn't ignorance of this due to men's being superstitious?

I want to speak plainly here. I say that if the people of the world want to partake of happiness, they must first destroy superstition; and, if the Chinese people want to enjoy happiness, they must first carry out a Confucian revolution. The destruction of human superstition in the world is the obligation of men in the world. The Chinese are a portion of the people of the world. The destruction of Chinese superstition is, in fact, the destruction of superstition among the people of the world. We are the Chinese people. . . .

How do we go about carrying out the Confucian revolution? Some people have proposed well-chosen expressions to abuse and attack him, but this would be an inefficacious way to proceed. When you consider the depth to which the Confucian poison has penetrated, if we don't employ the means of paring down to the bones to destroy the pox, then the joy of revival shall never be ours.

To my mind, the words and deeds of his lifetime can be classified in their entirety. His words can be sorted in the format of the *Donglai Zuo-shi boyi* (The extended meaning of the *Zuozhuan* by [Lü] Donglai [or Lü Zujian, 1137–81]) with stinging criticism added. His deeds could either refer to his daily activities, or be coupled with his words to censure him in such a way that he would have no room for maneuver. Unfortunately, my talents are limited, and I shall not be able to carry out this great task. However, if there is a man of good will whose mind is set upon saving the world, then I shall make all possible efforts to follow such a talented man even if I am unworthy.

The New Culture and Anti-Confucian movements of the May Fourth period are doubtless lineal descendants of this late Qing revolutionary group. Their call to categorize the words and deeds of Confucius with searing criticisms attached was successfully realized in the anti–Lin Biao, anti-Confucius campaign of the early 1970's. In the period prior to the 1911 Revolution, the anarchists were extremely busy introducing and spreading new scientific and scholarly ideas and, of course, deeply involved in their political activities; but, we do not see as much energy poured into attacks on Confucian morality or Confucius himself. The image of Confucius as a reactionary was still just beginning to be formed.

Conclusion

Let me summarize the points made in this essay as follows.

1. The issue of a Confucian religion arose in the late Qing as part of the reform and self-strengthening movements, but it was

also an end result of traditional Chinese scholarship. It was a search for roots that would enable China to unify as a "nation" before the imperialist invasion. The espousal of a Confucian religion by the reformers prompted a call against it from Zhang Binglin that was closely linked to the two sides' opposing scholarly views. Both groups took positions based in the *zhuzi* schools, and both played an important role in the revival of *zhuzi* writings.

2. Neither Kang Youwei's view of Confucius as the founder of a religion nor Zhang Binglin's view of him as a great figure in the ethnic culture of the Han people denied him a distinct position. Although their views divided over whether Confucius was to be the object of religious faith, both sides regarded him as worthy of reverence. However, the trend toward a genuine anti-Confucianism had emerged on the eve of the 1911 Revolution. It was to be found among the revolutionaries, among those who were affiliated with the socialists or anarchists. If one view of Confucius was anti-imperialist, then the argument of the anarchists and socialists at this time was an anti-imperialist position. If Kang Youwei's conception of Confucius and Confucianism is thought to be on the far right wing, then that of the socialists and anarchists would be on the far left; and Zhang Binglin's view would fall between them. In Kang's view, and in Zhang's for that matter, Confucius was the fount of China's distinctive *lijiao* (or *mingjiao*, rites and customs), and this was something that had to be defended. One camp among the revolutionaries went so far as to argue that *lijiao* itself was unacceptable and its prime mover was Confucius.

3. After the 1898 Reform Movement, Kang Youwei's support for a Confucian religion disappeared for a short while during the reform-vs.-revolution controversy.[73] The issue did not come up in the debate between the revolutionaries' organ *Minbao* and the reformers' *Xinmin congbao*. At the time of the founding of the Republic of China, though, arguments in favor of a Confucian religion began to reappear with renewed strength; a Confucian Association was established, and the movement it supported became active throughout China. Whether or not to articulate in the

constitution that China's national religion was Confucianism became the object of a social debate. Furthermore, Kang and his supporters aligned forces with Yuan Shikai's reactionary movement and formed a group clearly opposed to revolution. Opposition to them was aroused by the intellectuals led by Chen Duxiu (1879–1942) and the journal *Xin qingnian* (New youth). Influenced by the Russian Revolution and the May Fourth Movement, the Chinese Communist Party was founded, and thus was formed the great "anti-imperialist, anti-feudal" political movement.

One would have expected that within all these movements the issue of Confucius itself would have been an important point of contention. Opposition to Confucius, however, and to Confucianism lost its earlier significance in the broad ideological struggles of these movements. Perhaps in the anti-Confucius, anti–Lin Biao campaign of the early 1970's, anti-Confucianism has come to its end. Its founders were born in the anarchist and socialist sects of Tokyo and Paris during the era of the 1911 Revolution.

In this essay, I have discussed the issues of a Confucian religion, Confucius, and Confucianism, and I have tried to tease out their relation to the development of Qing scholarship and have tended to discuss them solely as issues in reformist and revolutionary ideology. As I noted at the outset of this essay, however, the issues dealt with here are closely entwined with the history of Chinese scholarship. Without investigating that aspect of the subject, a complete understanding would, I think, elude us. It is my hope and expectation that this article may play some role in supplementing that deficiency of past research.

Reference Matter

NOTES

Translator's note. Many of the writings of Zhang Binglin referred to in the notes that follow can now be found in *Zhang Taiyan quanji* (Collected works of Zhang Taiyan [Binglin]) (Shanghai: Renmin chuban she), of which six volumes have already been published with more expected: vols. 1 and 2, 1982; vol. 3, 1984; vols. 4 and 5, 1985; vol. 6, 1986. Abbreviated as QJ below.

1. *Zhang Binglin*

1. See the last part of his essay "Dao Han weiyan" (Subtle words of the great Han [people and culture]), and his article "Taiyan xiansheng zishu xueshu cidi" (Zhang Binglin's recounting of his own intellectual development), *Zhiyan* 25 (1936). Within *kaozhengxue*, Zhang was particularly enamored of Dai Zhen's philological work, which was noted for its theoretical rigor. As Zhang put it: "In their logical analyses, various scholars [such as Duan Yucai, Wang Niansun, Wang Yinzhi, Yu Yue, and Sun Yirang] of the same persuasion as Dai Zhen were meticulously strict. They returned to the past for ancient meanings and made judgments on the basis of earlier laws. In this they differed from the scholars of Suzhou [among whom Hui Dong was the founder]." "Qing ru" (Qing Confucians), *Jianlun* 4, in QJ 3: 472–80.

2. As a young man, Mao Zedong participated in a study society named for Wang, which was a great inspiration to him. See Kaizuka Shigeki, *Mō Takutō den* (Biography of Mao Zedong) (Tokyo: Iwanami shoten, 1959), pp. 11–13.

Translator's note. See also Frederic Wakeman, Jr., *History and Will: Philosophical Perspectives on the Thought of Mao Tse-tung* (Berkeley: University of California Press, 1975), pp. 82–83; and Stuart R. Schram, *Mao Tse-tung* (New York: Simon & Schuster, 1966), pp. 35–36, 60.

3. Ren Fangqiu, "Zhang Taiyan de xueshu sixiang yu geming jingshen" (Zhang Binglin's scholarly thought and revolutionary spirit), *Xin jianshe* (Feb. 1957), p. 21.

4. Hu Shi, "Wushi nian lai Zhongguo zhi wenxue" (Chinese literature over the past fifty years), appended to his *Guoyu wenxue shi* (A his-

tory of vernacular literature) (Shanghai: Xinyue shudian, 1928), pp. 269–80.

5. Wu Zhihui, "Huiyi Jiang Zhuzhuang xiansheng zhi huiyi" (Remembering Mr. Jiang Zhuzhuang's remembrances), *Dongfang zazhi* 33.1 (Jan. 1, 1936), p. 34.

6. *Translator's note.* Charlotte Furth gives 1902 as the first year of publication for *Qiushu*, which she translates as "Book of Raillery." See her "The Sage as Rebel: The Inner World of Zhang Binglin," in Charlotte Furth, ed., *The Limits of Change: Essays on Conservative Alternatives in Republican China* (Cambridge, Mass.: Harvard University Press, 1976), pp. 113, 375.

7. In *Guocui xuebao* (Aug. 1905), in *Taiyan wenlu* (Literary writings of Zhang Taiyan) 1; in QJ 4: 144.

8. In *Yayan* 7 (1914). Zhang's letters from this time have been published in *Zhang Taiyan xiansheng jiashu* (The family letters of Mr. Zhang Binglin) (Shanghai: Shanghai guji chuban she, 1985).

9. In Kita Ikki, *Shina kakumei gaishi* (The unofficial history of the Chinese Revolution) (Tokyo: Seiki shobō, 1921, rev. ed. 1941). Reprinted in *Kita Ikki chosakushū* (The writings of Kita Ikki), ed. Nomura Kōichi (Tokyo: Misuzu shobō, 1959), vol. 2. Kita also referred to Zhang as "a great sage who seemed ridiculous."

10. This is a chapter in Onogawa Hidemi, *Shinmatsu seiji shisō kenkyū* (Studies in late-Qing political thought) (Tokyo: Misuzu shobō, 1969), pp. 285–338. My essay was originally intended to supplement or expand on Onogawa's chapter on Zhang. I strongly urge readers to read his piece on Zhang along with mine.

11. Akutagawa Ryūnosuke, "Shanhai yūki" (Travels in Shanghai), included in his *Shina yūki*, in *Akutagawa Ryūnosuke zenshū* (Collected works of Akutagawa Ryūnosuke) (Tokyo: Iwanami shoten, 1977), pp. 28–30.

12. See Xu Guangping's afterword (dated June 25, 1937) to Lu Xun, *Qiejie ting zawen, mobian* (Miscellaneous notes from the Qiejie studio, final collection) (Shanghai: Shanghai renmin chuban she, 1973 reprint), pp. 149–50.

13. Zhang's speeches at the Academy have been collected in a pamphlet bearing the title *Zhang Taiyan baihua wen* (Zhang Binglin's vernacular writings), ed. Wu Zhairen (Shanghai: Taidong shuju, 1927); and *Zhang Taiyan de baihua wen* (Zhang Binglin's vernacular writings) (Taibei: Yiwen yinshuguan, 1972).

14. Some of the information contained in this citation was purposely left unclear by Lu Xun, and the blanks have been filled in by reference to Lin Chen, *Lu Xun shiji kao* (An examination of Lu Xun's biography) (Shanghai: Xin wenyi chuban she, 1955), p. 16.

Translator's note. This quotation generally follows the translation in *Selected Works of Lu Hsun* (Beijing: Foreign Languages Press, 1960), 4: 266–67, 269–70, with reference to the Chinese original and Shimada's Japanese translation to correct a number of errors. All transcriptions have been rendered in standard *pinyin*. The essay by Zhang referred to here as concerning "bilateral evolution" was "Jufen jinhualun" (Bilateral evolutionary theory), *Minbao* 7 (Sept. 5, 1906), pp. 1–14, in *Taiyan bielu* 2, in QJ 4: 386–94.

15. Zhou Xiashou (Zhou Zuoren), *Lu Xun de gujia* (Lu Xun's ancestral home) (Shanghai: Shanghai chuban gongsi, 1953), p. 347.

16. Xu Shoushang, *Wangyu Lu Xun yinxiang ji* (A collection of impressions of [our] departed friend, Lu Xun) (Shanghai: Emei chuban she, 1947), chap. 7 (pp. 27–31).

17. Zhang Binglin, "Shuolin" (A variety of ideas), part 1, *Minbao* 9 (Nov. 15, 1906), pp. 97–100, in *Taiyan wenlu* 1, QJ 4: 117–21. See also his "Wang Fuzhi congsi yu Yang Du can jiyao" (The essentials concerning Yang Du's participation in the prayers at the temple to Wang Fuzhi), *Minbao* 22 (July 10, 1908), pp. 40–44; "Shu Zeng ke Chuanshan ishu hou" (Letter following the publication of [Wang] Chuanshan's collected works by Zeng [Guofan]), in *Taiyan wenlu xupian* (Literary writings of Zhang Taiyan, continuation) 2, in QJ 5: 123–24; and "Jin si" (Recent thoughts), *Jianlun* 9, in QJ 3: 624–28.

18. "Shuolin," in QJ 4: 117–21.

19. Zhou Zuoren, "Xie ben shi" (Taking leave of my teacher), *Yusi* 94 (Aug. 28, 1926), pp. 275–76, written on Aug. 21, 1926.

20. See Lu Xun's letter to Cao Juren (dated June 18, 1933), in *Ro Jin senshū* (Selected works of Lu Xun), trans. Matsueda Shigeo (Tokyo: Iwanami shoten, 1956), 12: 164. The *touhu* incident occurred on Aug. 6, 1926.

21. See the speech Zhang delivered at the banquet in his honor in To-kyo, translated here in full; for citation, see note 27 below.

22. Lu Xun also noted: "The fence I build myself and that which I build with the help of others are separated in time."

23. *Translator's note.* See note 14 above (*Selected Works of Lu Hsun*, 4: 268–69).

24. Zhang Binglin, "Bozhong" (Scatter seeds), in *Qiushu* (old ed.), in QJ 3: 55–58.

25. Lin Chen, *Lu Xun shiji kao*, p. 21.

26. Lu Xun, "Wenhua pianzhi lun" (On the development of culture), in *Ro Jin senshū*, 5: 8–30.

27. Zhang Binglin, "Yanshuo lu" (Speech transcript), *Minbao* 6 (July 25, 1906), pp. 1–15.

28. The *Dong hua lu* is a comprehensive history of the Qing dynasty. The "incident" involving Dai Mingshi, Zeng Jing, and Cha Siting refers to the "literary inquisition" of the Qianlong Emperor. Widespread arrests and executions were carried out because it was claimed that these people had incurred the displeasure of the alien Qing house. Zheng Suonan was a Song loyalist after the Mongol invasion of China; Wang Chuanshan (Wang Fuzhi) was a Ming loyalist after the Manchu invasion.

Translator's note. I have translated *minzuzhuyi* as nationalism, although it should be noted that there was (and remains) a strong racialist flavor to the Chinese expression. The term *minzu* is best rendered (in this context) as race or ethnic group, although the latter is somewhat anachronistic, especially in English translation.

29. In fact, Zhang's sobriquet was Zhang Fengzi or Crazy Zhang. He also used the name Zhang Yangxian or Zhang the Epileptic, as he apparently often had seizures.

30. *Translator's note.* Even Shimada has no idea what this refers to. I can only join him in throwing up my hands.

31. This contains a sarcastic jibe in the direction of Kang Youwei and his followers. Zhang's point was that by advocating protection of the emperor and affirming the Manchu dynasty then in place, the reformers were longing for wealth and success and that this had been the peculiar nature of the Gongyang (New Text) school ever since the Han dynasty.

32. The text between the quotation marks in this sentence reads *Guzhi guwei*, which was the name of a book by Wang Renjun (1866–1913) published in 1896. *Guzhi* carries the meaning of "natural science." The [more complex expression] *guwei* indicates the effort to derive everything in Western natural science from China, with citations to ancient Chinese classical sources.

33. The "nine principles" is short for "three laws and nine principles." In addition to the theory of the three ages (*sanshi*) of history, the Gongyang school also argued a theory that there were "three unifications" (*santong*), and a theory that distinguished inner and outer. To-

gether, these constituted the "nine principles." For a more detailed discussion see Ojima Sukema, *Chūgoku no kakumei shisō* (Chinese revolutionary thought) (Tokyo: Chikuma shobō, 1967), pp. 112–31; and the section on Liu Fenglu in Kano Naoki, *Chūgoku tetsugaku shi* (A history of Chinese philosophy) (Tokyo: Iwanami shoten, 1975), esp. p. 623.

34. *Translator's note.* For a similar citation from the work of Dai Zhen, see Benjamin A. Elman, *From Philosophy to Philology: Intellectual and Social Aspects of Change in Late Imperial China* (Cambridge, Mass.: Council on East Asian Studies, Harvard University, 1984), p. 18.

35. "Taiyan xiansheng zishu xueshu cidi"; and Zhu Xizu, *Taiyan xiansheng koushou biji* (Notes dictated by Professor Zhang Taiyan).

36. "Xian zengzu xundaojun xianzu guozijun xiankao zhixian shilüe" (Brief biographies of my late great-grandfather, grandfather, and father), in *Taiyan wenlu xupian* 4, in QJ 5: 196.

37. Lu Xun touched on this in "A Few Matters Connected with Zhang Taiyan," *Selected Works of Lu Hsun*, vol. 4.

38. Many of Zhang's articles written at this time are collected in *Gujing Jingshe keyi qiji* (Seven essay collections of selected topics from the Gujing Jingshe), comp. Yu Yue (n.p., 1895), 12 *juan*.

39. Wei Yuan, "Wujin Li Shenqi xiansheng zhuan" (A biography of Li Shenqi [Zhaoluo] of Wujin), in *Guweitang waiji* (Outer chapters from the Guweitang) (Taibei: Wenhai chuban she, 1969 reprint of 1878 orig.), *juan* 4.

40. Gong Zizhen, "Hang dazong yishi zhuang" (Statement concerning the extraordinary circumstances surrounding the great Hang), in *Dingan wenji bubian* (Supplement to the literary writings of [Gong] Dingan [Zizhen]) (Shanghai: Commercial Press, 1929 reprint of 1886 orig.), *juan* 4, pp. 11a–12b.

41. *Translator's note.* Kojō Teikichi (1866–1949) was trained as a Sinologist in his native Kumamoto prefecture before being sent to China as a journalist at the end of the nineteenth century. Trapped there at the time of the Boxer Uprising, he discovered and was able to save a portion of the *Yongle dadian* (Yongle encyclopedia) during the destruction brought on by the invasion of the joint expeditionary forces. In 1901 he returned to Japan to teach at the forerunner of Takushoku University; in 1906 he began teaching at Tokyo University, where he remained until 1938. He was a renowned bibliophile, especially of Chinese texts, and a prolific scholar.

42. Yet despite a number of rhetorical flourishes, one should look, for example, at the confession in his introduction to *Buxing er yanzhong*

buting ze guowang (Unfortunately, my warnings have come true. If no one heeds me, the nation will perish) (Shanghai: Changxing, 1918).

43. Tan Sitong, *Tan Sitong quanji* (The collected works of Tan Sitong) (Beijing: Sanlian shudian, 1954), p. 58, *passim*.

44. *Xinhai geming* (The Revolution of 1911) (Shanghai: Shanghai renmin chuban she, 1957), 1: 378.

45. Yongjia is a place name, Chen's hometown, which came to be associated with a school of thought contemporary with Zhu Xi. It had more of a historical and political bent than a philosophical one.

46. "Bozhong," *Qiushu* (old ed.), in QJ 3: 55–58. In general, however, his discontent with respect to Tan's writings and ideas was more striking.

47. "Qing gu Longan fuxue jiaoshou Liao jun muzhi ming" (Epitaph to Liao [Ping], former teacher at the Longan prefectural school in the Qing era), in *Taiyan wenlu xupian* 5.2, in QJ 5: 264–65.

48. Zhang later drew this contrast as one between constitutionalism and racialism.

49. "Mingji" (Hearts are united as one without speaking), *Qiushu* (old ed.), in QJ 3: 29–31; "Shangyang" [Lord Shang], *Qiushu* (old ed.), in QJ 3: 79–82.

50. Zhang subsequently became dissatisfied with the *Zuozhuan du* and did not publish it. Apparently, only his "Shulu" (Explanatory notes) to the *Chunqiu Zuozhuan du* (Reading the *Zuo Commentary* on the *Spring and Autumn Annals*) and his "Liu Zizheng Zuoshi shuo" (Liu Zizheng [Liu Xiang] on the *Zuozhuan*) were published. However, I have been able to examine an edition of *Chunqiu Zuozhuan du* (9 *juan*, bound in one volume) published in 1939, after Zhang's death, by Pan Chengbi (held in the private collection of Professor Yoshikawa Kōjirō). According to Pan's introduction, the book was originally published widely in a small-sized edition.

Translator's note. This volume has now been reprinted in QJ 2: 1–804; "Shulu" appears in QJ 2: 805–66.

51. Kano Naoki, *Chūgoku tetsugaku shi*, p. 616.

52. These are nonetheless the views of late-Qing *Zuozhuan* scholars and revolutionaries. The most convenient, schematic way to understand the rivalry in the late Qing between revolution and reform would be as follows:

Zuozhuan — Old Text school — "nationalism" — revolution
Gongyang — New Text school — constitutionalism — reform

Yet there are several points in this particular case worthy of note. First, the *Zuozhuan* or Old Text school, as shown above, emerged in opposition to the Gongyang school; it was not the reverse at all. Second, for all the essential points of both the *Zuozhuan* and the *Gongyang Commentary*, or the schools of thought they spawned for that matter, certain doubts may be raised about the view that *Zuozhuan* scholars would become racialist revolutionaries and Gongyang scholars would become internationalist, constitutionalist reformers. Several historical facts are worth citing:

a. Studies of the *Gongyang Commentary* on the *Spring and Autumn Annals* initially arose as a regular branch of *kaozhengxue* during the Qing period. See, for example, Kong Guangsen's (1752–86) *Chunqiu Gongyang tongyi* (Comprehensive meaning of the *Gongyang Commentary* on the *Spring and Autumn Annals*), included in the massive compendium *Huang Qing jingjie* (Qing exegeses of the classics).

b. By subsequently adopting He Xiu's explanation of the *Gongyang Commentary* in particular, the Gongyang school began to demonstrate its strikingly intellectual and historical philosophical qualities (as in the case of the Changzhou school of Liu Fenglu, among others). It went beyond simple classicism, seeking to function as a social and political trend of thought (as in the case of such men as Gong Zizhen).

c. Finally, the Gongyang school emerged, as summarized in the diagram above, with Kang Youwei and Liang Qichao.

d. In rebellion, Zhang Binglin especially emphasized the racialist revolutionary quality of the *Zuozhuan*. Only then did the Zuozhuan school materialize in the sense outlined above. Among its adherents were Zhang, Liu Shipei, and others.

53. See Kano Naoki, *Chūgoku tetsugaku shi*; and Ojima Sukema, *Chūgoku no kakumei shisō*, pp. 109–15.

54. Zhang Binglin, "Pai-Man pingyi" (Level-headed discussion of anti-Manchuism), *Minbao* 21 (June 10, 1908), pp. 1–12, in *Taiyan bielu* (Additional writings of Zhang Taiyan) 1, in QJ 4: 262–70.

55. Onogawa Hidemi, *Shinmatsu seiji shisō kenkyū*, p. 417.

56. See his "Yu ren lun puxue baoshu" (Letter to others discussing pure textual scholarship), in *Taiyan wenlu* 2, in QJ 4: 153–54; and "Yuan jing" (On the classics), in *Guogu lunheng* (Disquisitions on the national heritage) (Taibei: Guangwen shuju, 1967 reprint of Shanghai orig., n.d.), *zhongjuan* (middle section), pp. 79–95.

57. "Yuan ren" (On human beings), in *Qiushu* (old ed.), in QJ 3: 21–

24; however, when this essay later appeared in *Jianlun* (in QJ 3: 356–60), his earlier classification of China and Japan together changed to a joint classification of India and Jiaozhi (an antique name for what is today northern Vietnam), from which Japan was expunged.

58. For a period of time, Sun and Zhang broke off their relationship altogether.

59. Pi Xirui, *Jingxue lishi* (A history of classical scholarship) (Shanghai: Commercial Press, 1934); (Hong Kong: Zhonghua shuju, 1961 reprint); and (Taibei: Wenhai chuban she, 1964 reprint).

60. Wei Yuan, *Guweitang waiji*, *juan* 4. See also Zhang Binglin's "Xueyin" (Studying eremitism), in *Jianlun*, in QJ 3: 480–81, and in the addendum to *Jianlun*, in QJ 3: 111–12.

61. See Su Yu, "Changxing xue ji" (Notes on education in Changxing), in *Yijiao congbian* (The Yijiao collection of essays), comp. Ye Dehui (Taibei: Wenhai chuban she, 1971 reprint of Wuchang orig., 1898), pp. 239–300.

62. See Liu Shipei, *Zuoan waiji* (Inner collection of Zuoan), *juan* 9, in his *Liu Shenshu xiansheng yishu* (Collected works of Mr. Liu Shenshu [Shipei]), (n.p., 1934–36).

63. In this connection, Zhang had his own distinctive theory of "statecraft" (*jingshi*) ideas, expressed in such works of his as "Chunqiu jingshi xianwang zhi zhi" (The will of the former kings who brought order to the realm in the Spring and Autumn period). See "Chunqiu guyan" (Former words on the *Spring and Autumn Annals*), in *Jianlun*, in QJ 3: 407–12; and "Yuan jing," in *Guogu lunheng*, *zhongjuan*, pp. 79–95.

64. "Zhuzi xueshuo lüe" (Outlines of the theories of the *zhuzi*), *Guocui xuebao* 20 (7/20/1906).

65. See "Yu ren lun puxue baoshu," in *Taiyan wenlu* 2, in QJ 4: 153–54; and "Guanzhi suoyin" (A guide to the bureaucracy), *Minbao* 14 (June 8, 1907), pp. 1–21, in *Taiyan wenlu* 1, in QJ 4: 86–99.

66. Apparently, Spencer had attacked the trivialism of empirical historiography for trying to prove something as unimportant as the fact that "next door, a cat gave birth to a kitten." Although I am unacquainted with this citation, it appears in *Zhang Taiyan baihua wen*, and later Lu Xun used it in this same sense.

67. "Da Tie Zheng" (Response to the letter of Tie Zheng), *Minbao* 14 (June 8, 1907), pp. 113–22, in *Taiyan wenlu bielu* 2, in QJ 4: 368–75.

68. "Zun shi" (Respect for history), in *Jianlun*, in QJ 3: 413–20; also in *Jianlun*, in QJ 3: 356–60; and "Si xiangyuan" (Thinking of *xiangyuan*), in *Taiyan wenlu* 1, in QJ 4:129–37.

69. "Chunqiu guyan," in *Jianlun*, in QJ 3: 407–12.

70. "Ai fenshu wushi ba" (Sorrow for the burning of 58 books), in *Qiushu* (new ed.), in QJ 3: 322–24. By the "tearing up" of documents, Zhang is pointing here to the banning of books or the elimination of certain characters from books on a large scale in cases where such works were deemed unfavorable to the Qing.

71. "Yuan jing," in *Guogu lunheng, zhong juan*, pp. 79–95.

72. "Yindu zhongxing zhi wang" (India's hope for a revival), *Minbao* 17 (Oct. 25, 1907), pp. 99–103, in *Taiyan bielu* 2, in QJ 4: 360–63.

73. "Yindu ren zhi lun guocui" (Indians' views of national essence), *Minbao* 20 (April 15, 1908), pp. 35–37, in *Taiyan bielu* 2, in QJ 4: 366–67.

74. See the entry under "Daojia" (Daoists), in "Zhuzi xueshuo lüe," *Guocui xuebao* 20 (7/20/1906).

75. "Ding Kong" (Correcting Confucius), in *Jianlun*, in QJ 3: 423–27; this passage is missing from the text of "Ding Kong" as it appears in *Qiushu* (new ed.), in QJ 3: 134–36.

76. "Yu ren lun puxue baoshu," in *Taiyan wenlu* 2, in QJ 4: 153–54.

77. "Bo jianli Kongjiao yi" (Refutation of the petition to establish a Confucian religion), in *Taiyan wenlu* 2, in QJ 4: 194–98.

78. Traditionally, the Chinese divided all written works into four categories: *jing* (classics), *shi* (history), *zi*, and *ji*. The *zi* classification included intellectual and theoretical works; the *ji* classification included literary works.

79. Zhang Xuecheng, "Bao Sun Yuanru shu" (Responding to Sun Yuanru's letter), in *Wenshi tongyi* (General principles of literature and history) (Beijing: Guji chuban she, 1956 reprint), "outer chapter" 3, p. 312.

80. "*Nanjiang yishi* xu" (Preface to the *Unofficial History of the Southern Reaches*), in *Taiyan wenlu* 2, in QJ 4: 201–2.

81. "Qing ru" (Qing Confucians), in *Jianlun*, in QJ 3: 472–80.

82. One can speak of Yuhang and Hangzhou as Eastern Zhejiang in a broad sense. The traditions of the Eastern Zhejiang school go back at least to the Song dynasty.

83. "Yu Sun Zhongrong shu" (Letter to Sun Zhongrong [Yirang]), in *Taiyan wenlu* 2, in QJ 4: 162–63.

84. For Zhang, the word "classics" (*jing*) was not a particularly estimable designation, and he demonstrated that originally the term signified a "written work." See "Yuan jing," in *Guogu lunheng, zhong juan,* pp. 79–95.

85. See Zhang's speech "Lun jingshi shilu buying wugu huaiyi" (Since the classics and the histories are facts, one must not doubt them without reason; an analysis), appended to his *Guoxue gailun* (Outline of national learning), ed. Cao Zhuren (Hong Kong: Chuangken chuban she, 1953), pp. 122–24; and Zhu Zuqiu's article in *Zhiyan* 25 (1936), p. 6. Although Qian Xuantong had been a disciple of Zhang's ever since their years in Tokyo, he later became fascinated by Kang Youwei's book *Xinxue weijing kao* (A study of the forged classics of the Xin period) and became a champion of the "doubters of antiquity," a group of historians who brought new methods to the study of ancient Chinese texts.

86. *Guocui xuebao* 21 (8/20/1906), and subsequent issues (later included in his *Guogu lunheng, zhong juan,* pp. 39a–44b).

87. For an overall picture of Zhang's notion of "national learning," useful works include the aforementioned *Guoxue gailun* (first publ. 1922); *Guoxue lüeshuo* (Brief discussion of national learning) (Hong Kong: Xianggang huanqiu wenhua fuwu she, 1963), Zhang's lectures compiled by Sun Shiyang; and "Taiyan xiansheng zishu xueshu cidi."

88. See Huang Jie's remarks in the inaugural issue of *Guocui xuebao* 1 (1/20/1905).

89. "Yindu ren zhi lun guocui," *Taiyan bielu* 2, in QJ 4: 366–67.

90. "Yuan xue" (On learning), in *Guogu lunheng, xiajuan,* pp. 147–55.

91. "Yi wang" (A discussion of kingship), in *Jianlun,* in QJ 3: 457–61.

92. "Yu Luo Zhenyu shu" (A letter to Luo Zhenyu), in *Taiyan wenlu* 2, in QJ 4: 171–73.

93. "Liuxue de mudi he fangfa" (The aim and method of overseas study), in *Zhang Taiyan de baihua wen,* pp. 1–13.

94. This view was widely held. See Zhang's essay "Daiyi ranfou lun" (On the applicability of representative government), *Minbao* 24 (Aug. 10, 1908), pp. 1–27, in QJ 4: 300–311.

95. Ojima Sukema, *Chūgoku no kakumei shisō,* pp. 113–16.

96. The tendency to try to read extraordinary and deep meaning into this "Buddhist voice" in Zhang's essays has become pronounced in recent studies of Zhang Binglin in Japan. Thus, the tendency not to take

an overall view of Zhang and consider his relationship to the entire history of Chinese thought and scholarship, to magnify Zhang's views (virtually without limit, indeed uncontrollably) in this particular area, and to draw some sort of bizarre conclusion from all this has become marked.

If one were to expand the point at issue here at random, a variety of conclusions could be read into one part of Zhang's argument and deductively expanded to fill his entire thought: Zhang as evidence that the people themselves were not understood by the emperor or the local gentry; Zhang as revolutionary advocating the abolition of the literati class; Zhang regarding China at the time of the Revolution of 1911 as a bloc of people blank and empty (in a positive sense), but opposed to the intrusion of outsiders and aware of the need for self-preservation (hence, a force of resistance), a view consistent with Mao Zedong's conceptions of China and "the people"; Zhang as a thinker opposed to "modernization" who, from the position of the people at the very base of an ancient structure, sought to negate modernization together with that structure. Perhaps one may reach such conclusions; as Mencius ("Gaozi," *xia*) once said: "If you bring the tips to the same level without measuring the difference in the bases, you can make a piece of wood an inch long reach a greater height than a tall building."

Nonetheless, to argue that this or that constitutes the thought of Zhang Binglin is rather bewildering. The work of intellectual history, when for example studying a certain thinker, is to follow the twists and turns that this thinker's ideas genuinely describe. This means a recognition of the fact that one is depicting those turns, even the not-so-sharp ones, for while a thinker may have been full of the potentialities to move along numerous tangential directions, the actual course followed is never consistent. Attributing to Zhang the thesis that the Chinese people "are empty and blank in a positive sense" may not be impossible, if one takes a limited portion of Zhang's writings and piles deduction on top of deduction. How in the world, however, can we link the Zhang Binglin indicated by this view—which has, in fact, been argued—with the Zhang Binglin who bragged about China's "national essence" and boasted of Chinese civilization, as we have tried to describe him in this essay? Is this any different from contemporary Chinese historians who deplore Zhang's praise of the greatness of Chinese civilization of the past, which, they argue, had nothing to do with the common people? To say that Zhang's position was "populist" or tied to the common people, no matter what one thinks, is a bit too abstruse an explanation.

Perhaps this is analogous to the point Zhang made in the speech translated above that all the policies of the Chinese dynasties were socialist. Yet how can we possibly say such a thing and have it accord with the following statement made by Zhang?

"My idea of a government is most assuredly not that of the 'parliamentary system.' When I was in Japan, I wrote a piece entitled 'Daiyi ranfou lun' (On the applicability of representative government). Even if our national polity (*guoti*) should become democratic, I do not wish to transform our social practices. Nor do I wish to change our institutions altogether. I base these views on the principle of no sudden changes in history"(*Taiyan xiansheng zishu xueshu cidi*).

The Greek philosopher Thales derived the theory that nothing is born of nothing from the expression "Water is eternal" [i.e., that water is the source of all else]. Hegel later noted that a certain historian of philosophy [J. J. Brucker] said that Thales was "amongst the philosophers who deny creation from nothing" (*Introduction to the Lectures on the History of Philosophy*, trans. T. M. Knox and A. V. Miller, Oxford, Clarendon Press, 1985, p. 105). His point was that "many different views and conclusions that can be deduced cannot be argued or considered in the least." I shall never forget this point, and it applies not only to views of Zhang Binglin. One often comes across "studies" of Chinese intellectual history in Japan [and elsewhere] in which deduction has substituted for argument.

One of the major characteristics of Zhang's thought, especially in the period when he established his "Buddhist voice," was what is often called romantic irony. One definition of romantic irony points to thought's capacity to fly (*Fliegenkönnen*). Yet, Zhang's essay "Wu wu lun" (On the five negations), which has been praised to the skies in recent studies of Zhang—his advocacy of the eradication of government, of population centers, of humanity, of living creatures, and of the world (*Minbao* 16, Sept. 25, 1907, pp. 1–22, in *Taiyan bielu* 2, in QJ 4: 429–43)—is a typical example of this romantic irony. Of course, I do not believe that one can begin any sort of deduction immediately by attaching such a general category to it, but in any event I thought this point ought to be made at the outset. Furthermore, Zhang said that the "theory of limitless revolution . . . could offer a critique from the perspective on the other side of infinity that would make such a revolution even more thoroughgoing." However, if in arguing about the length of a pencil, one used logic to deal with a "light year," there was "nothing to fear." I do not necessarily feel that such logic is meaningless, for under certain circumstances at certain stages it might even be absolutely necessary. But, in the case of Zhang Binglin, to overestimate it would surely be dangerous.

Zhang often spoke of differentiating "ideas of pure ultranationalism" from immediate necessity. The former, as in the case of his notion of the five negations, always lay at the root of one's personality or thought and, right or wrong, did not seem to me to play the decisive factor in determining the latter. Especially when you introduce the perspective of Zhang Binglin after the establishment of the Republic, this scarcely makes any sense at all. Rather, what strikes me as a major problem is why Zhang adopted such an excited "Buddhist voice" (I use this expression in an abstract sense) in this period. For the time being, let me bring this particular argument to a close with two conclusions. The way Zhang's thought has been characterized by recent commentators, first of all, fails to understand his thought in the most general sense of the expression—namely, as one would go about understanding the thought of Confucius or Kant. Second, in a more limited sense, such commentators fail to understand Zhang's thought in the period when he was editor of *Minbao* (1906–8), the high point of his activities as a revolutionary.

The recent studies of Zhang Binglin to which I have been referring include primarily Nishi Junzō, "Mu kara no keisei" (Formation from nothing), *Tenbō* 71 (Nov. 1964), pp. 44–55; and Kondō Kuniyasu, "Shō Heirin ni okeru kakumei shisō no keisei: Bojutsu henpō kara Shingai kakumei e" (The formation of Zhang Binglin's revolutionary thought, from the 1898 Reform Movement to the 1911 Revolution), *Tōkyō daigaku Tōyō bunka kenkyūjo kiyō* 28 (March 1962), pp. 207–64. Several years ago, I made similar comments in "Shō Taien shisō kenkyū zakkan" (Impressions drawn from research on the thought of Zhang Taiyan), *Chūgoku kindai shisō shi kenkyū kaihō* 23 (March 1962), pp. 177–78.

97. Ma Xulun, "Taiyan xiansheng ziding nianpu biyi" (Supplement to Mr. Zhang Binglin's chronological autobiography), *Jindai shi ciliao* 1 (Jan. 1958), pp. 138–41.

98. In addition, Zhang wrote the following articles about India for *Minbao*: "Song Yindu Boluohan Baoshen erjun xu" [Preface sent to two Indian gentlemen, Boluohan and Baoshen], *Minbao* 13 (May 5, 1907), pp. 97–100, in QJ 4: 358–60; "Yindu zhongxing zhi wang" (India's hope for a revival), *Minbao* 17 (Oct. 25, 1907), pp. 99–103, in QJ 4: 360–63; "Yindu duli fangfa" (Ways for India to gain independence), *Minbao* 20 (April 25, 1908), pp. 31–32, in QJ 4: 363–64; "Yindu ren zhi guan

Riben" (Indians' view of Japan), *Minbao* 20 (April 25, 1908), pp. 32–35, in QJ 4: 364–65; "Yindu ren zhi lun guocui" (Indians' views of national essence), *Minbao* 20 (April 25, 1908), pp. 35–37, in QJ 4: 366–67; and "Zhina Yindu lianhe zhi fa" (A way for China and India to unite), *Minbao* 20 (April 25, 1908), pp. 37–39, in QJ 4: 367–68.

99. Kang Youwei, *Buxing er yanzhong buting ze guowang*, p. 36.

100. For an article on this subject in Chinese, see Ding Zeliang, "Zhang Binglin yu Yindu minzu jiefang douzheng" (Zhang Binglin and the Indian people's liberation struggle), *Lishi yanjiu* (Jan. 1957), pp. 25–40.

101. *Translator's note.* Zhang transcribed the names of these two Indians into Chinese, and I have been unable to uncover their names in Roman script. The Chinese pronunciation for Mr. A is Boluohan; for Mr. B, it is Baoshen. The latter may be a Chinese approximation of Bashem.

102. Tian Heng was the last king of the state of Qi. He resisted Gaozu of the Han dynasty [Liu Bang] until the very end and then committed suicide. The Haoli was the name of his funeral dirge.

103. "Yindu ren zhi guan Riben," *Minbao* 20 (April 25, 1908), pp. 32–35, in QJ 4: 364–65.

104. "Song Yindu Boluohan Baoshen erjun xu," *Minbao* 13 (May 5, 1907), pp. 97–100, in QJ 4: 358–60.

I have scarcely been able to trace Zhang Binglin's activities in the history of the socialist movement at the beginning of the twentieth century. See Takeuchi Zensaku, "Meiji makki ni okeru Chū-Nichi kakumei undō no kōryū" (Exchanges between the Chinese and Japanese revolutionary movements in the late-Meiji period), *Chūgoku kenkyū* 5 (Sept. 1948), p. 86. I highly recommend Takeuchi's detailed essay for its remarkable reminiscences. He vividly describes at length the Shakaishugi kōshūkai (Socialist Lecture Society) and the Ashū washinkai (Asian Friendship Society) of Kōtoku Shūsui, Sakai Toshihiko, Yamakawa Jun, Ōsugi Sakae, and others. For an essay of this sort, there are surprisingly few clerical errors. There is just one I would like to point out, concerning Huang Zongxi's *Mingyi daifang lu* as the basis of Zhang's thought. As I noted earlier, once Zhang became conscious of himself as a revolutionary, he went out of his way to denounce the *Mingyi daifang lu*, which was the bible of the reformers, and ultimately he reviled Huang Zongxi as a shameless scoundrel. However, in China Zhang has in many instances inadvertently been regarded as an exponent of the *Mingyi daifang lu*, a significant fact that we should keep in mind.

2. Confucius in the 1911 Revolution

1. Beijing daxue Ru-Fa douzheng shi bianxie xiaozu, zhexue shehui kexue jichu duwu (Compilation group for the history of the Confucian-Legalist struggle, Beijing University, basic reading material in philosophy and social science), *Ru-Fa douzheng shi gaikuang* (Outlines of the history of the Confucian-Legalist struggle) (Beijing: Renmin chuban she, 1973), p. 120. This originally appeared in *Beijing daxue xuebao* 6 (1974). For the sources cited within this quotation, see Qi Zhongjiu, *Taiping tianguo de fan-Kong douzheng* (The anti-Confucian struggle of the Taiping Heavenly Kingdom) (Beijing: Wenwu chuban she, 1974); and Tang Xiaowen, *Laodong renmin fan-Kong douzheng jianshi* (A short history of the anti-Confucian struggle of the working people) (Beijing: Renmin chuban she, 1974).

2. The transmission of legends about the Taiping Rebellion as an anti-Manchu nationalist (pro-Han Chinese) struggle have become widely known with the memoirs of Sun Zhongshan and Zhu De (1886–1975). However, on the question of anti-Confucianism, one scarcely sees mention of Taiping anti-Confucianism even at the time of the anti-Confucian movement of the May Fourth period.

3. See "Goshi undō tsugu mono, Shū shushō Kōshi hihan ni genkyū" (A continuation of May Fourth, Premier Zhou [Enlai] comments on the critique of Confucius), *Asahi shinbun* (Jan. 5, 1974), p. 4.

4. Zhu Yixin, *Wuxie tang dawen* (Response from the Hall of Righteousness) 2 (Taibei: Guangwen shudian, 1969 reprint of 1892 orig.), entry on the "Bibliographic Treatise" in the *Hanshu* (History of the [Former] Han dynasty).

5. On Wang Zhong's study of the *Mozi*, see Yoshikawa Kōjirō, "Nit-Chū shoshigaku shakugi" (An exposition of studies of the *zhuzi* in Japan and China), in *Yoshikawa Kōjirō zenshū* (Collected works of Yoshikawa Kōjirō) (Tokyo: Chikuma shobō, 1973), 2: 474–97; and Shimada Kenji, "Shinchō makki ni okeru gakumon no jōkyō" (The state of scholarship in the late Qing period), in *Kōza. Chūgoku, II: Kyū taisai no Chūgoku* (Symposium. China, II: China under the old regime), ed. Yoshikawa Kōjirō (Tokyo: Chikuma shobō, 1967), pp. 250–84.

Translator's note. Citations come from Wang Zhong, *Shuxue, neipian* (Discourses on learning, inner chapters) (Taibei: Guangwen shuju, 1970 reprint), 3: 1a–4a; and Weng Fanggang (who criticized Wang so harshly), *Fuchuzhai wenji* (Literary collection from the studio of the return to beginnings) (n.p., 1877 ed.), 15: 9a. See Elman, *From Philosophy to Philology*, pp. 76–78, 278.

6. Liang Qichao, *Qingdai xueshu gailun* (Outlines of Qing scholarship), trans. Immanuel C. Y. Hsü, *Intellectual Trends of the Ch'ing Period* (Cambridge, Mass.: Harvard University Press, 1959), p. 87.

7. Kano Naoki, *Ryō Kan gakujutsu kō* (An examination of scholarship in the two Han dynasties) (Tokyo: Chikuma shobō, 1964), sec. 15, "Kanseitei no setsu" (The theory of the miraculous births of emperors), pp. 154–60, and sec. 16, "Kanseitei to shite no Kōshi" (Confucius as a case of imperial miraculous birth), pp. 160–65. See also Kano's *Chūgoku tetsugaku shi* (A history of Chinese philosophy) (Tokyo: Iwanami shoten, 1975), section on Liu Fenglu (1776–1829), pp. 623–32.

8. Zou Boqi, "Xueji yide" (An advantage to the study of calculations) (1844).

9. Qian Hansheng, "Qingmo de 'Xiyang yuanchu Zhongguo' shuo" (The late-Qing theory that the West originated in China), *Lingnan xuebao* 4.2 (June 1935), pp. 57–102. See also Zhang Binglin's speech at the meeting welcoming his release from prison, translated above.

10. I shall not touch in this essay on the issue of those who [allegedly] performed this crushing to death, but the school of Xunzi (the Zhu Xi school should also be included here), which stressed ritual, is what is being referred to. See Liang Qichao, "Lun Zhina zongjiao gaige" (On religious reform in China), in his *Yinbing shi heji, wenji* (Collected writings from an ice-drinker's studio, literary writings) (Shanghai: Zhonghua shuju, n.d.), 2: 54–61; several of Liang's essays, including this one, are translated in my *Chūgoku kakumei no senkushatachi* (Pioneers of the Chinese Revolution) (Tokyo: Chikuma shobō, 1970), pp. 5–59; Tan Sitong, *Renxue* (On Benevolence), *xia*, trans. Ono Shinji, in *Kakumei ronshū* (Essays on revolution), ed. Ono Shinji, Yoshida Fumio, and Hazama Naoki (Tokyo: Asahi shimbun sha, 1972), vol. 15 of the *Chūgoku bunmei sen* (Selections from Chinese civilization) series, pp. 20–61.

11. Since I cut my analysis short here and it may seem abrupt, let me add a bit at this point. The third conception of Confucius—as an enlightenment figure—was clearly not the result of *kaozhengxue*, but of contact with Western imperialist civilization, the "Western impact." I lumped this image with the other two as the consequences of *kaozhengxue* because I am arguing from the position of a logical development in which the issue of Confucius is intrinsic to the history of traditional scholarship in China. Thus, I may have rounded off the edges a bit. Since the import of the "Western impact" is discussed in the body of this essay, I hoped to deal with the issue in this way. I wanted to emphasize that, even before the "Western impact," factually and logically

the transformation of Confucius into a *zhuzi* had already begun as a consequence of the unfolding of Chinese scholarship itself. Of course, without a blasting cap, explosives are not likely to explode. But I am examining the explosives here in discussing the causes of the explosion. While I would not deny that the "Western impact" played a role in the form the explosives took or in facilitating their explosion, I think the essential elements of these explosives should be dealt with first and foremost.

12. Kang Youwei, "Wuxu zou kao" (Draft memorial of 1898; first actually published in May 1911), in *Wuxu pianfa* (The 1898 Reform Movement) (Shanghai: Shanghai renmin chuban she, 1957), vol. 3. A complete translation (by Ono Kazuko) of the memorial can be found in *Shinmatsu Minkokusho seiji hyōron shū* (Collection of political commentaries from the late Qing and early Republican Periods), ed. Nishi Junzō and Shimada Kenji (Tokyo: Heibonsha, 1971), pp. 55–60. At the time the present essay was being proofread, I came across Huang Zhangjian's book *Wuxu bianfa shi yanjiu* (A study of the history of the 1898 Reform Movement) (Taibei: Zhongyang yanjiuyuan lishi yuyan yanjiusuo, vol. 54, 1970). Huang argues that of the 25 sections contained in Kang's "Draft Memorial of 1898," only two are acceptable as actually written in 1898; the others are later forgeries (or massive rewrites) done by Kang himself. Thus, the text of the memorial concerning the Confucian religion is a forgery. This was a truly astonishing claim, but I could not help feeling that the evidence cited was far too arbitrary. At present, though, I do not have the energy for a rebuttal, and I shall have to accept his point. Accordingly, I should have had no choice but to revise this essay, which assumed Kang's memorial to be genuine, but I came into possession of Huang's book only after this essay left my hands. Since I could not change the text, I have had to add this little commentary as a note.

Fortunately, the main aim of this portion of my essay is a general discussion of Kang Youwei's and the reformers' views of Confucius and of a Confucian religion. Thus, even if this memorial did not exist in the year 1898, this fact presents no fundamental obstacle. Even if it is a forgery, it is Kang Youwei's forgery and clearly provides an exposition of views on a Confucian religion in the Memorial of Provincial Graduates (1895). It had to have been forged between 1898 and May 1911, i.e., the eve of the 1911 Revolution, and this still makes it possible to understand Liang Qichao's argument on the nonimmediacy of a Confucian religion, which we shall examine presently. Thus, if we can take this as the approved version of Kang Youwei's views on a Confucian religion on the eve of the 1911 Revolution, our analysis thus far remains completely plausible, and our immediate necessity is satisfied.

If I might add just one more point, even if portions of Kang's "Draft Memorial of 1898" have been changed, it would surely not be an absurd conjecture to suggest that a memorial whose essential point was the need for a Confucian religion (probably as a national religion) may have existed in the sixth month of the 24th year of the Guangxu reign and that portions of the "Draft Memorial of 1898" may have been "forged" as a basis for it.

13.   By a Confucian dating system, this year of Guangxu 24 (1898) would have been 2449. When Kang wrote of "making Confucius the equal of Heaven," he had in mind the worship of Confucius going hand in hand with worship of Heaven. In his 1913 "Petition to Make Confucianism the National Religion and to Place [Confucius] on a Par with Heaven," Kang wrote: "We shall reverence the Temple of Heaven and construct the Mingtang [temple used in the Zhou for sacrifices to the Lord on High]. At the ceremony for the winter solstice at the Temple of Heaven and at the ceremony for the Lord on High at the Mingtang, we must treat Confucius as the equal of the Lord on High. In these two ceremonies, the head official will lead the many other officials in performing the rites, and in the localities where they have built temples for prayer to heaven, they shall use these for treating Confucius on an equal footing. Schools have often made use of former Confucian temples, but here it would be best to lay central emphasis on the Lord on High, and Confucius can be taken as his equal." According to the foregoing, in the case of schools (referred to as *xuegong*) Kang argued that, while the principle deity would be heaven (the Lord on High), the places of worship were probably "Confucian temples." Was the same true of local schools as well? Were there not both temples for prayer to heaven (in which Confucius was now also to be placed) and temples for Confucius (alone)?

14.   Ichiko Chūzō, "Hokyō to henpō" (Protect the faith and reform), in Ichiko Chūzō, *Kindai Chūgoku no seiji to shakai* (Modern Chinese politics and society) (Tokyo: Tokyo University Press, 1971), pp. 222–45; Onogawa Hidemi, "Kō Yūi no henpōron" (Kang Youwei's views on reform), in Onogawa Hidemi, *Shinmatsu seiji shisō kenkyū* (Studies in late Qing political thought) (Tokyo: Misuzu shobō, 1969), pp. 86–156; and Nomura Kōichi, *Kindai Chūgoku no seiji to shisō* (Modern Chinese politics and thought) (Tokyo: Chikuma shobō, 1964), sec. 1, chap. 4.

15. Liang Qichao, "Lun Zhina zongjiao gaige," in *Yinbing shi heji, wenji*, 2: 54–61.

16. Ibid.

17. Chen Hanzhang, "Kongjiaohui xu" (Introduction to the Confucian church), written in Oct. 1912, in *Kongjiaohui zazhi* 1.1 (Feb. 1913), pp. 1–7.

18. *Zhuangzi*, "Tianzufang," in *The Complete Works of Chuang Tzu*, trans. Burton Watson (New York: Columbia University Press, 1968), p. 227. The rough figures preceding this citation were Kang's effort to prove Zhuangzi's statement mathematically.

19. The term used here in the *Hunan Shiwu xuetang chuji* (First collection from the Shiwu Academy of Hunan) is *jingjiao* (luminous religion), which refers to Christianity.

Translator's note. Jingjiao was the term for Christianity found on the eighth-century Nestorian tablet in Shaanxi.

20. *Lunyu* (Analects [of Confucius]), "Zizhang," 23; following Arthur Waley, trans., *The Analects of Confucius* (New York: Vintage, 1938), p. 229.

21. *Lunyu*, "Zihan," 12 and "Gongye," 6; Waley, pp. 141, 108.

22. *Zhongyong* (Doctrine of the mean), 31.4.

23. *Wuxu bianfa*, 4: 505; also included in Liang Qichao, *Yinbing shi wenji*, vol. 2. The final few sentences concerning the tasks of spreading the faith are not to be found in *Hunan Shiwu xuetang chuji*. This ideal of evangelizing Confucianism throughout the world was originally Kang Youwei's; see Onogawa Hidemi, *Shinmatsu seiji shisō kenkyū*, p. 194.

24. Liang Qichao, *Qingdai xueshu gailun*, chap. 26; trans. slightly modified from Hsü, *Intellectual Trends of the Ch'ing Period*, p. 106.

25. Liang Qichao, "Baojiao fei suoyi zun Kong lun," in *Yinbing shi heji, wenji*, 4: 50–59. See also Onogawa Hidemi, "Shinmatsu no shisō to shinkaron" (Late-Qing thought and the theory of evolution), in *Shinmatsu seiji shisō kenkyū*, p. 270; and Ichiko Chūzō, "Ryō Keichō no henpō undō" (Liang Qichao in the 1898 Reform Movement), in *Kindai Chūgoku no seiji to shakai*, p. 255.

26. *Lunyu*, "Zihan," 7, and "Shuer," 21; Waley, pp. 127, 140.

27. *Mengzi* (Mencius), "Wanzhang," *xia* (pt. 2), I, 5.

28. Of course, this is not to say that Liang Qichao never mentioned the Confucian religion or Confucius at a later date. For example, in a note in the final portion of an essay entitled "A Discussion of the General Trend of Changes in Chinese Scholarly Thought," he wrote: "People engaging in the new learning of late generally consider it a positive qual-

ity to attack Confucius. But once the road to freedom of thought has been cleared, even if going too far may be inevitable, today it is quite clear that two thousand years of ancient texts cannot be allowed to shackle our national thought, nor can the doctrines of Confucius be allowed to impede our progress. What benefit would there be in that? Furthermore, one or two eminent scholars are hostile to Confucius because the Confucian religion is based on the unit of the family; and it was Confucius who made our nation suffer for such a long time with a lineage-based society and made us incapable of developing a national society. Also, Confucius entrusted authority in a sovereign, and it was Confucius who enabled these enemies of the people to use this authority for two thousand years as a charm. One cannot deny their point here, but it only applies to Confucius's doctrine of *xiaokang* or 'ascending peace' [the second in the three stages of Kang Youwei's three historical eras leading to *datong* or 'great harmony']. Why do they not pay attention to Confucius's teaching of *datong*, when the world will belong to all men? Doesn't this only benefit the enemies of the people? While a people's psychology many initially be at rest, it can achieve unity and make orderly progress."

It is not known to whom Liang was referring by "one or two eminent scholars," but he probably would have included Zhang Binglin among them. Liang, "Lun Zhongguo xueshu sixiang bianqian zhi dashi" (A discussion of the general trend of changes in Chinese scholarly thought), *Xinmin congbao* 12 (Dec. 1904), pp. 39–55.

29. Sun Zhongshan, "Minzuzhuyi" (Nationalism), lecture six in *Sanminzhuyi* (Three principles of the people).

30. As an example of this, I would point to Sun's article "Ping Shi Still Does Not Affirm Recognition of His Errors," which appeared in the Singapore newspaper *Zhongxing ribao* in 1908. This piece is important for the light it sheds on Sun's intellectual formation.

31. See Chen Tianhua's testament (in Japanese translation) in Shimada Kenji, "Aru kakumeika no isho" (The testament of a revolutionary), in *Chūgoku kakumei no senkushatachi*, p. 77.

32. In Shimada Kenji and Ono Shinji, eds., *Shingai kakumei no shisō* (The thought of the 1911 Revolution) (Tokyo: Chikuma shobō, 1968), p. 218.

33. *Translator's note.* The reason Shimada refers to Zhang's action as one of recoining an expression is that the term Zhang used, *guoxue* or national learning, already had a long history in Japan (peaking in the eighteenth century). *Kokugaku*, as the term is pronounced in Japanese,

usually refers to a movement of the mid-Tokugawa period when nativist scholars began reacting against the predominance of Chinese learning in Japanese scholarship. Thus, in Japan, "national learning" was a call for a return to things Japanese and away from things Chinese; in the way Zhang and others used the expression in China, "national learning" was a reaction against the dominance of all things foreign, especially Western, and a call for a return to things Chinese. Since all of this is widely known to educated readers in Japan, Shimada could elide the discussion with a quasi-pun.

34. For what follows concerning Zhang Binglin and his *Qiushu*, see Onogawa Hidemi, "Shō Heirin to hai-Man shisō" (Zhang Binglin and anti-Manchu thought), chap. 8 of *Shinmatsu seiji shisō kenkyū*, pp. 285–338; Takata Atsushi, *Shō Heirin Shō Shichō Ro Jin* (Zhang Binglin, Zhang Shizhao, Lu Xun) (Tokyo: Ryōkei shosha, 1974). Recently a study was published on the formative process of Zhang's thought, based on a detailed analysis of the drafts, marginal notations, and the like of Zhang's *Qiushu*. See Yang Zhijun, "Cong *Qiushu* de xiuding kan Zhang Taiyan de sixiang yanbian" (Changes in Zhang Taiyan's thought as seen from the revised edition of *Qiushu*), *Wenwu* 234 (Nov. 1975), pp. 59–74; but it has no bearing on the main points I make here.

Translator's note. Both editions of the *Qiushu* can now be found in QJ, vol. 3.

35. *Mengzi*, "Gongsun chou," *shang*, II, 24.

36. *Lunyu*, "Yongye," 1; Waley, p. 115.

37. Zhang Binglin, "Ru xia," in *Jianlun*, in QJ 3:438–42.

38. This passage follows with some modification a short piece by Xin Li, "Shi 'jiuwang' bushi 'jiuzai': guanyu 'Ding Kong' yijiulingwu nian ban de yige cuozi" (It was "jiuwang," not "jiuzai": An incorrectly written character in the 1905 edition of [Zhang's essay] "Ding Kong"), *Lishi yanjiu* (April 1975), p. 116.

39. Zhang Binglin, "Zhuzi xueshuo lüe," *Guocui xuebao* 20 (7/20/1906).

40. *Translator's note.* Professor Shimada may have placed the revival of common knowledge about Zhang Xuecheng and his work a bit early. There certainly was renewed interest in Zhang in the very first years of the twentieth century, but by 1906 (when this essay by Zhang Binglin was written) I doubt one can say that Zhang Xuecheng's ideas were widely known among Chinese intellectuals. We do know that Zhang Binglin was well aware of his namesake's writings. I have tried to sort out the details of the revival of Zhang Xuecheng in "On the 'Rediscov-

ery' of the Chinese Past: Ts'ui Shu and Related Cases," in *Perspectives on a Changing China: Essays in Honor of Professor C. Martin Wilbur on the Occasion of His Retirement* (Boulder, Colo.: Westview, 1979), pp. 230–32.

41. The Six Classics were works of history for Zhang Binglin. Precisely because works of history recorded facts, they could nicely foster in the Chinese people a "sense of nation" (*guoxing*). See the first essay translated in the volume.

42. *Lunyu*, "Zihan," 12; Waley, p. 141.

43. *Zhuangzi*, "Dao Zhi" (Robber Zhi), following Burton Watson, pp. 324–25.

44. *Lunyu*, "Weizi," 8; Waley, p. 222.

45. *Zhongyong* 2, citing Confucius.

46. See note 27 above.

47. *Lunyu*, "Zilu," 20; Waley, p. 176.

48. *Lunyu*, "Yanghuo," 13; Waley, p. 213.

49. Attributed to the Song Emperor Zhenzong (r. 998–1023), in *Guwen zhenbao* (Treasury of old texts).

50. See the essay devoted to Zhang Binglin, translated in the volume.

51. In *Yayan* 1 (Dec. 1913), in *Taiyan wenlu* (Literary writings of Zhang Taiyan) 2, in QJ 4: 94–98.

52. *Yijing*, diagram "Guan."

53. *Lunyu*, "Bayi," 11; Waley, p. 96.

54. *Laozi*, 26.

55. The major objective of the movement for a Confucian religion in the Republican period was to specify in the constitution of the Republic of China the one item that would "make Confucianism the national religion" of China. Thus, Zhang was introducing here constitutions from various countries in the world that specified a national religion (Chile, Switzerland, and the like).

56. Gongshuzi or Gongshu Ban was a well-known craftsman from the state of Lu, mentioned in *Mencius*, "Lilou," part 1, I.1; Xuanyuan was a name given to the Yellow Emperor because it is believed he hailed from a place once so named in present-day Henan province; and Xiao He (d. 193 B.C.E.) was a meritorious official of the first Han emperor, Gaozu (r. 206–195 B.C.E.)

57. *Translator's note.* Bo Yi and Liuxia Hui are mentioned several times in the *Mencius*. Perhaps Zhang was referring to the passage from *Mencius*, "Jinxin," part 2, XV: "Mencius said, 'A sage is the teacher of a hundred generations—this is true of Bo Yi and of Liuxia Hui.'"

58. The New Text school deeply revered Dong Zhongshu, and Kang Youwei wrote a work entitled *Chunqiu Dongshi xue* (Mr. Dong [Zhongshu]'s study of the *Spring and Autumn Annals*).

59. *Liji*, "Quli."

60. *Lunyu*, "Shuer," 1.

61. When the issue of a national religion was raised by the committee to draft a constitution, it was initially rejected for inclusion in the text of the constitution because making Confucianism a national religion, it was argued, contradicted the principle of a republic of five peoples. The pro-religion group wholeheartedly opposed this. See Kang Youwei, "Kongjiaohui xu" (Introduction to the Confucian church), *Kongjiaohui zazhi* 1.2 (March 1913), p. 1; and Kongjiao zonghui (General Confucian church), "Letter to Comrades Throughout the Land Respectfully Concerning Denial of a National Religion by the Committee to Draft the Constitution," *Kongjiaohui zazhi* 1.9 (Oct. 1913). The latter piece argued that "we have heard false reports of a rebellious Mongol King Wutai. . . . We have recently heard of a movement in China to abolish the Confucian religion. How can it be that the Confucian religion is about to be abolished and Buddhism is well protected? . . . No one in the world can be expected to dislike the founder of his own religion, nor does anyone love and respect the founder of another religion." The article went on to argue that even if a national religion were established, Buddhism in Mongolia and Tibet ought to be recognized as in the past according to the principle of freedom of religion. Zhang is here arguing in opposition to this point. Furthermore, the reason the article refers to a "rebellious king" of Inner Mongolia is that on Nov. 11, 1912, this king proclaimed: "Because I want Buddhism to be protected, I shall submit my allegiance at Urga." See Wu Zongci, ed., *Zhonghua minguo xianfa shi* (A history of the constitution of the Republic of China) (n.p.: Dongfang shibao guan, 1924), p. 53.

62. "Biography of Xiang Xu," *Hou Hanshu* (History of the Later Han dynasty).

63. Kang Youwei's idea of a Confucian religion apparently included, to a certain extent, advocating and implementing the destruction of Buddhist temples, Daoist monasteries, and sites of sacrificial offerings, and the like, or their conversion into schools.

64. Wu Yu, "Ming Li Zhuowu lingzhuan" (An informal biography of Li Zhuowu [Li Zhi] of the Ming), reprinted in *Wu Yu wenlu* (Writings of Wu Yu) (Shanghai: Yadong tushuguan, 1921), *xia*, pp. 20–51.

65. In response to an essay by Liu Yizheng, entitled "A Discussion

of the Errors Made by Modern Scholars in Analyzing the Schools of the Thought of the *Zhuzi*" (*Shidi xuebao* 1.1), Zhang wrote in 1922 (in the same journal): "This major piece of work is critical of my earlier thesis [contained in the section on the Daoists in "Zhuzi xueshuo lüe"], which claimed that 'Confucius stole the library supervised by Laozi and feared disclosure. . . .' I put this crazy conjecture forth over ten years ago . . . and I went so far as to doubt the sagacity of the sage. This essay was carried by *Minbao* [Zhang's error; it appeared in *Guocui xuebao*], but I have already had it expunged from my collected works, *Zhangshi cangshu*. As a greenhorn shedding my first skin, I never dreamed I would be saying this now. My mind has endured your scathing criticism, and I thank you" (*Shidi xuebao* 1.4 [1922]).

66. Saitō Akio and Niijima Atsuyoshi, *Chūgoku gendai kyōiku shi* (A history of contemporary education in China) (Tokyo: Takabatake, 1973), p. 72.

67. Jiang Liangqi, *Dong hua lu* (Records from within the Eastern Flowery Gate), Guangxu reign, "Bingwu" day, 11th month, 1904; printed in book form, *Qinding xuetang zhangcheng*. See also Chen Qingzhi, *Zhongguo jiaoyu shi* (A history of Chinese education) (Taibei: Taiwan shangwu yinshu guan, 1963); Saitō Akio and Niijima Atsuyoshi, *Chūgoku gendai kyōiku shi*; and Hattori Unokichi, *Kōshi oyobi Kōshikyō* (Confucius and the Confucian religion) (Tokyo: Kyōbunsha, 1926), pp. 118ff.

68. *Dong hua lu*, Guangxu reign, "Wuchen" day, 3d month, 1907.

69. *Dong hua lu*, Guangxu reign, "Wushen" day, 11th month, 1907.

70. The entire article appears in *Tianyi* 3 (July 10, 1907), pp. 7–23; 5 (Aug. 10, 1907), pp. 65–70.

Translator's note. On He Zhen, see Ono Kazuko, *Chinese Women in a Century of Revolution, 1850–1950*, ed. Joshua A. Fogel (Stanford, Calif.: Stanford University Press, 1989), pp. 66–68, 70, 217–18.

71. *Xin shiji* 11 (Aug. 31, 1907), pp. 1–2.

72. *Xin shiji* 52 (June 20, 1908), p. 4.

73. In his chronological biography of Liang Qichao, Ding Wenjiang notes that in the Republican period Chen Huanzhang, a leader in the Association for the Confucian Religion, proposed the formation of an Association to Propagate the Religion in New York (July 1907). He quotes a letter from Chen to Liang: "From the very start, Mr. Nanhai [i.e., Kang Youwei] lacked the energy to carry through his advocacy of the religion. . . . In February of this year, I entered Columbia University in New York. . . . On Kang's occasional visits to New York, he

often sought my advice about whether he should talk primarily about politics or about religion. I responded that it would be best if he would talk about both. He said he was unable to do both, and that he had recently received a letter from London indicating that this problem remained undecided. I still think he has to do both because there has to be a revolution in the Chinese political realm as well as in the religious realm." Ding Wenjiang, *Liang Rengong xiansheng nianpu changpian chugao* (Draft chronological biography of Mr. Liang Rengong [Qichao]) (Taibei: Shijie shuju, 1972), entry for July, Guangxu 33 (1907).

CHARACTER LIST

Ai 哀

Ajia rekishi kenkyū nyūmon アジア歴史研究入門

Akutagawa Ryūnosuke 芥川龍之介

Bailun 白論

Ban Gu 班固

"Baojiao fei suoyi zun Kong lun" 保教非所以尊孔論

bian 變

"Bo Kang Youwei lun geming shu" 駁康有為論革命書

"Bo Kongjiao jianli yi" 駁孔教建立議

Bo Yi 伯夷

Bolan fenmie ji 波蘭分滅記

Cai Yuanpei 蔡元培

Cha Siting 查嗣庭

Chan (Zen) 禪

Chang Ju 長沮

Chen Dongshu 陳東塾

Chen Duxiu 陳獨秀

Chen Fuchen (Jieshi) 陳黻宸 (介石)

Chen Huanzhang 陳換章

Chen Li 陳澧

Chen She 陳涉

Chen Sheng 陳勝

Chen Tianhua 陳天華

Chen Zhongzi 陳仲子

Cheng Hao 程顥

Cheng Weishi lun 成唯識論

Cheng Yi 程頤

Chengyun tu 成韵圖

Chūgoku ni okeru kindai shii no zasetsu 中國に於ける近代思惟の挫折

chunfeng meisu 醇風美俗

Chunqui Dongshi xue 春秋董事學

Chunqiu Gongyang tongyi 春秋公羊通議

Dacheng qixin lun 大乘起信論

dafu 大父

Dai Dongyuan de zhexue 戴東原的哲學

Dai Mingshi 戴名世

Dai Zhen 戴震

"Daiyi ranfou lun" 代議然否論

daoxue 道學

Dazai Shundai 太宰春台

dazhuan 大篆

di 弟

"Ding Kong" 訂孔

Ding Wenjiang 丁文江

Dong hua lu 東華錄

Dong Zhongshu 董仲舒

Donglai Zuoshi boyi 東萊左氏博議

Dongshu dushu ji 東塾讀書記

Du You 杜佑

Duan Yucai 段玉裁

"Dusheng (xia)" 獨聖 (下)

E da Bide bianzheng zhi 俄大彼得變政志

Erya 爾雅

Erya yishu　爾雅義疏

Faguo geming ji　法國革命記

Fangyan　方言

"Fei Kong weiyan"　廢孔微言

"Fen"　墳

fengzi　瘋子

fu　父

Fu Sheng　伏生

Fujino Genkurō　藤野嚴九郎

Futang riji　復堂日記

Gaozu　高祖

"Geming daode lun"　革命道
　德論

Geming jun　革命軍

gezhi　格致

Gong Chong　宮崇

Gong Zizhen　龔自珍

gongche shangshu　公車上書

Gongshu Ban　公輸班

Gongshuzi　公輸子

Gongsun Long　公孫龍

Gongyang zhuan　公羊傳

gongzhu　共主

Gu Jiang　顧絳

Gu Jiegang　顧頡剛

Gu Tinglin　顧亭林

Gu Yanwu　顧炎武

Gu Zuyu　顧祖禹

Guangyun　廣韻

"Guimao yuzhong ziji"　癸卯
　獄中自記

Gujing jingshe　詁經精舍

guocui　國粹

Guocui xuebao　國粹學報

Guogu lunheng　國故論衡

guogu zhengli　國故整理

guoti　國體

guoxing　國性

guoxue　國學

guoxue dashi　國學大師

guoyuan　國愿

guwei　古微

Haiguo tuzhi　海國圖志

Hang Shijun　杭世駿

Hao Yixing　郝懿行

Haoli　蒿里

He Xiu　何休

He Zhen　何震

Hong Xiuquan　洪秀全

"Hongfan"　洪範

Hu Shi　胡適

Hua-Xia　華夏

Huan　桓

Huang Jie　黃節

Huang Kan　黃侃

Huang Qing jingjie　皇清經解

Huang Shisan　黃式三

Huang Xing　黃興

Huang Yizhou　黃以周

Huang Zonghui　黃宗會

Huang Zongxi　黃宗羲

Huang Zongyang　黃宗仰

Huangshu　黃書

Huayan　華嚴

Hufa　護法

Hui Dong　惠棟

Ji　季

ji　集

"Ji Yindu Xipoqi wang ji'nianhui
　shi"　記印度西婆耆王記念
　會事

Jia Yi　賈誼

jiajie　假借

jian'ai　兼愛

Jiang Liangqi　蔣良騏

jiangsheng　講生

Jianlun　檢論

jiao　教

jiaobu　教部

Jiaozhi　交趾

Jiaozhou tongyi 校讎通義

jiaozhu 教主

Jie Ni 桀溺

jingjiao 景教

jingshi (statecraft) 經世

jingshi (teacher of classics) 經師

jingtian 井田

Jingyi shuwen 經義述聞

Jiyun 集韻

"Jue sheng" 絕聖

jun 君

juntian 均田

juren 舉人

Kang Youwei 康有為

kaozheng 考証

kaozhengxue 考証學

"Kedi" 客帝

"keqing" 客卿

Kinkikan 錦輝館

Kita Ikki 北一輝

Kojō Teikichi 古城貞吉

Kong Guangsen 孔廣森

Kongzi gaizhi kao 孔子改制考

Lan Gongwu 藍公武

Leipian 類篇

li (distance) 里

li (principle) 理

li (propriety) 禮

Li Linfu 李林甫

Li Si 李斯

Li Shizeng 李石增

Li Zhaoluo 李兆洛

Li Zhi 李贄

Li Zhuowu 李卓吾

Li Zicheng 李自成

Liao Ping 廖平

Liji 禮記

"Liqi" 禮器

Lishu tongyi 禮書通義

lisu 禮俗

Liu Bang 劉邦

Liu Bannong 劉半農

Liu Fu 劉復

Liu Ji 劉基

Liu Shipei 劉師培

Liu-Song 劉宋

Liu Xiang 劉向

Liu Xin 劉歆

Liu Yu 劉欲

Liu Yuxi 劉禹錫

Liu Zijun 劉子駿

"Liu Zijun sishu dizi" 劉子駿私淑弟子

Liu Zhiji 劉知幾

Liuxia Hui 柳下惠

lixue 理學

Longhuahui 龍華會

Lu Xiangshan 陸象山

Lu Xun shiji kao 魯迅事蹟考

Lü Zujian 呂祖儉

"Lun Zhongguo zongjiao gaige" 論中國宗教改革

Lunheng 論衡

Luo Taishan 羅台山

Luo Yougao 羅有高

Ma Duanlin 馬端臨

Ma Xulun 馬叙倫

Ma Yucao 馬欲藻

Mengzi ziyi shuzheng 孟子字義疏証

Minbao 民報

Mingyi daifang lu 明夷待訪錄

minzu 民族

minzuzhuyi 民族主義

Miura Baien 三浦梅園

Miyake Yūjirō (Setsurei) 三宅雄二郎(雪嶺)

Miyazaki Tōten 宮崎滔天

"Moxue tonglun" 墨學通論

Mozi xiangu 墨子閒詁

Naitō Konan　內藤湖南
Nakae Chōmin　中江兆民
"Nanhai Kang Xiansheng
　zhuan"　南海康先生傳
"Nüzi fuqiu lun"　女子復仇論
Ogyū Sorai　荻生徂徠
Ojima Sukema　小島祐馬
Ōkuma Shigenobu　大隈重信
Onogawa Hidemi　小野川秀美
palai paqu　爬來爬去
Pan Chengbi　潘承弼
Peng Chimu　彭尺木
Peng Shaosheng　彭紹升
Pi Xirui　皮錫瑞
pingminzhuyi　平民主義
puxue　樸學
qi　氣
Qi wu lun shi　齊物論釋
Qian Daxin　錢大昕
Qian Xuantong　錢玄同
Qiangxuehui　强學會
qicui　齊衰
Qilüe　七略
Qin Shi Huangdi　秦始皇帝
"Qing ru"　清儒
qingjing　清靜
Qiushu　訄書
Qu Yuan　屈原
Quan Zuwang　全祖望
Quanxue pian　勸學篇
Ren Fangqiu　任訪秋
Renxue　仁學
Riben Mingzhi bianzheng kao
　日本明治變政考
ru　儒
"Ru bing"　儒兵
"Ru Dao"　儒道
"Ru Fa"　儒法
"Ru Mo"　儒墨

"Ru xia"　儒俠
Ruan Yuan　阮元
rujia　儒家
rusheng　儒生
rushu　儒術
"Sangang geming"　三綱革命
Sanlun　三論
sanshi　三世
santong　三統
Sanzang fashi bashi guiju lun zan
　三藏法師八識規矩論贊
Seiyōken　精養軒
Shang Yang　商鞅
shangding　上丁
Shangshu　尚書
Shao Jinhan　邵晋涵
Shao Zhenmao　少正卯
Shaojun　少君
Shen Buhai　申不害
shengyuan　生員
shi (deed, fact)　事
shi (history)　史
shi (regional mentor)　師
shi (serviceman)　士
Shi Qiu　史鰌
Shiermenlun　十二門論
Shiga Shigetaka　志賀重昂
Shimada Kenji　島田虔次
Shiming　釋名
*Shin juka tetsugaku ni tsuite, Yū
　Juriki no tetsugaku*　新儒家哲學
　について、熊十力の哲學
Shina yūki　支那游記
Shinmatsu seiji shisō shi kenkyū
　清末政治思想史研究
shishi　師氏
shishi qiushi　實事求是
Shitong　史通
Shiwu　時務

Shiwubao 時務報
shixue 史學
"Shō Heirin no minzoku shisō"
　　章炳麟の民族思想
shu 術
Shun (emperor) 順
Shushigaku to Yōmeigaku
　　朱子學と陽明學
Sima Guang 司馬光
Sima Tan 司馬談
situ 司徒
siyi 四裔
Song Heng 宋衡
Song Pingzi 宋平子
Song Shu 宋恕
Su Manshu 蘇曼殊
Subao 蘇報
Sun Chuanfang 孫傳芳
Sun Yirang 孫詒讓
Sun Zhongshan 孫中山
Tachibana Shiraki 橘樸
Taishang ganying pian 太上感
　　應篇
Tan Sitong 譚嗣同
Tan Xian 譚獻
Tang (Mrs., king) 湯
Tang Zhen 唐甄
Tao Zhu 陶朱
Tian Heng 田橫
tianfu 天府
Tiantai 天台
tianxia wei gong 天下為公
Tianyi 天意
Tongdian 通典
Tongzhi 通志
touhu 投壺
Tujue shoujiu xiaorou ji 突厥
　　守舊削弱記
Wan 皖

Wan Sida 萬斯大
Wan Sitong 萬斯同
Wang Chong 王充
Wang Chuanshan 王船山
Wang Fuzhi 王夫之
Wang Gen 王艮
Wang Niansun 王念孫
Wang Xianqian 王先謙
Wang Yangming 王陽明
Wang Yinzhi 王引之
Wang Zhong 王中
wangdao 王道
Wei Yuan 魏源
Weishi 唯識
weiyan dayi 微言大義
Wenchang dijun yinzhi wen
　　文昌帝君陰隲文
Wencheng 文成
"Wenshi" 文始
Wenshi tongyi 文史通義
Wenxian tongkao 文獻通考
Wenxin diaolong 文心雕龍
"Wenxue lun lüe" 文學論略
Wu Chengshi 吳承仕
"Wu wu lun" 五無論
Wu Yu 吳虞
Wu Zhihui 吳稚暉
Wuli 五利
xia 俠
Xia Zengyou 夏曾佑
xiangfen 相分
xiangyuan 鄉愿
Xiangzong luosuo 相宗絡索
Xiao He 蕭何
xiaokang 小康
xiaoxue 小學
xiaozhuan 小篆
Ximing 西銘
xin 心

"Xin fangyan" 新方言

Xin shiji 新世紀

Xin Weishi lun 新唯識論

Xin xue weijing kao 新學偽經考

xinglixue 性理學

Xinmin congbao 新民叢報

xiong 兄

Xiong Shili 熊十力

Xiong Tingbi 熊廷弼

xiongdi 兄弟

Xu Guangping 許廣平

Xu Shoushang 許壽裳

Xuan Yuan 軒轅

xue 學

xuegong 學宮

Xunzi jijie 荀子集解

Yang Cihu 楊慈湖

Yang Renshan 楊仁山

Yang Wenhui 楊文會

Yang Xuangan 楊玄感

yi 義

Yi Dun 猗頓

yidi 夷狄

yin 尹

Yinming ruzheng lilun 因明入正理論

Yinxue wushu 音學五書

yinyang 陰陽

Yishu 義疏

Yokoi Shōnan 橫井小楠

Yongle dadian 永樂大典

Yoshikawa Kōjirō 吉川幸次郎

youshuo 游說

Yu Quyuan 俞曲園

Yu Yue 俞樾

yuan 円

Yuan Huang 袁黃

Yuan Liaofan 袁了凡

Yuan Rang 原壤

Yuan Shikai 袁世凱

Yue Fei 岳飛

Yuelu 嶽麓

"Yugong" 禹貢

Yujia shi di lun 瑜伽師地論

Yujia shi di lunzhu 瑜伽師地論註

Yupian 玉篇

Zeng Guofan 曾國藩

Zeng Jing 曾靜

zhancui 斬衰

Zhang Binglin 章炳麟

Zhang Daoling 張道陵

Zhang Fengzi 章瘋子

Zhang Hengju 章橫渠

Zhang Ji 張繼

Zhang Juzheng 張居正

Zhang Shizhao 章士釗

Zhang Taiyan 章太炎

Zhang Xianzhong 張獻忠

Zhang Xingyan 章行嚴

Zhang Xuecheng 章學誠

Zhang Xueliang 張學良

Zhang Yangxian 章羊癇

Zhang Zai 張載

Zhang Zhidong 張之洞

Zheng Qiao 鄭樵

Zheng Sixiao 鄭思肖

Zheng Suonan 鄭所南

Zheng Xuan 鄭玄

Zhi 跖

Zhonggong (Ranyong) 仲弓 （冉雄）

Zhonglun 中論

Zhou Zuoren 周作人

Zhouli zhengyi 周禮正義

Zhu Ciqi 朱次琦

Zhu De 朱德

Zhu Xi 朱熹

Zhu Xizi 朱希祖

Zhu Youqian　朱有虔
Zhu Youquan　朱有泉
Zhu Zonglai　朱宗萊
zhuanzhu　轉注
zhuzi baijia　諸子百家
Zhuzi pingyi　諸子平議
"Zhuzi xueshuo lüe"　諸子學說略
Zigong　子貢

Zisang Bozi　子桑伯子
Zisi　子思
Zizhi tongjian　資治通鑑
Zou Rong　鄒容
"Zun Xun"　尊荀
Zuo Qiuming　左丘明
Zuo Zongtang　左宗棠
Zuozhuan du　左傳讀

INDEX

In this index an "f" after a number indicates a separate reference on the next page, and an "ff" indicates separate references on the next two pages. A continuous discussion over two or more pages is indicated by a span of page numbers, e.g., "57–59." *Passim* is used for a cluster of references in close but not consecutive sequence. Entries are alphabetized letter by letter up to the first punctuation mark.

France, 81, 102, 137, 141
Freedom of religion, 100–101, 103, 167
Freedom of thought, 94
Fujino Genkurō, 22
Furth, Charlotte, 146
Fu Sheng, 126–27
Futang riji, 53
Fuxi, 124

Gaozu, 158, 166
"Geming daode lun," 76
Geming jun, 18, 23
Geometry, 94
Germany, 30, 33f, 102
Golden Age, 94–95
Golden Mean, 99, 119
Gong Chong, 127
Gongshuzi (Gongshu Ban), 125f, 166
Gongsun Long, 123
Gongyang school, *see* New Text / Gongyang school
Gongyang zhuan, 7–8, 49–57 passim, 92–93, 100, 121, 151
Gong Zizhen, xi, 151
Gorky, Maxim, 26
Government: parliamentary, 14, 74f, 156; and Confucius, 32, 133–38 *passim*; Zhang Binglin and, 32, 35–36, 39–40, 74f, 156; India and, 35–36, 63, 75. *See also* Constitutionalism; Democracy; Monarchy; *individual dynasties*
Great Learning, xi, 108
Greece, 80f
Guangdong, 21
Guangxu reign, 97f, 162
Guangyun, 38
Guanzi, 112
"Guimao yuzhong ziji," 19
Gu Jiegang, 70
Gujing Jingshe, 46–49, 53, 68
Guocui xuebao, 72f, 75, 115–16
Guogu lunheng, 16

Guomindang, 24–25
Guoxue, see "National learning"
Guoyuan, 60, 119
Gu Yanwu (Tinglin, Jiang), 5–6, 43–47 *passim*, 59, 121–22
Guzhi guwei, 148
Gu Zuyu, 59

Haiguo tuzhi, 58
Han dynasty, 4, 87, 97, 158, 166; Later, 4, 7, 40, 123, 127; Former, 7f, 32, 58, 60, 92, 115f; Zhang Binglin and, 32, 38, 40–42, 58ff, 71, 113, 118, 126–27, 148
Hanfeizi, 94, 123
Hanfeizi, 8, 13, 52
Hang Shijun, 48
Hangzhou, 46, 153
Han learning, *see Kaozhengxue*
Han people: Zhang Binglin and, 18, 25, 28ff, 36–37, 44ff, 56f, 75, 140; and barbarians, 54–55, 56
Hanshu, 62; "Bibliographic Treatise," 65, 91, 115, 117, 120
Haoli, 80, 158
Hao Yixing, 47
Hegel, G. W. F., 94, 156
He Xiu, 54, 151
He Zhen, 137
History: *kaozhengxue* and, 6, 59, 66, 70; Confucius/Confucianism and, 8, 60–66 *passim*, 88–90; Zhang Binglin and, 38–39, 60–72 *passim*, 128, 152; India and, 63–64, 75
"Hongfan," 126
Hong Xiuquan, 88
Huan, Duke of Qi, 114
Huang Kan, 14f
Huang Qing jingjie, 47
Huang Shisan, 68
Huangshu, 52–53
Huang Xing, 16, 108
Huang Yizhou, 66, 68
Huang Zhangjian, 161

Huang Zonghui, 12
Huang Zongxi, 12, 43, 50, 52f, 59, 66f, 75f, 158
Huang Zongyang, 13, 18
Huayan Buddhism, 11f, 34–35, 113
Hufa (Protect the Constitution) Army, 21
Hui Dong, 58, 145
Huizhou (Waichow) Uprising, 49
Hundred Days Reform Movement, *see* Reform Movement
Hundred Schools, 8, 91, 94–95; Zhang Binglin and, 10, 42, 65, 71, 112, 117, 120, 129. *See also Zhuzi*
Hu Shi, 15–16, 65

Idealism, xiii–xiv, 12
Illiteracy, 14, 104
"Imperial Educational Guidelines," 135–36
Imperialism, 75, 102f, 140, 160
"Imperial Regulations on Schools," 134–35
Independence movement, Indian, 63–64, 76–83
India: and Buddhism, 35–36, 66, 75, 78, 80, 124; Zhang Binglin and, 35–36, 42, 63–64, 73–83 *passim*, 152, 157–58
Institutions: Zhang Binglin and, 39–41, 72. *See also* Government; School system
"Internationalism," 56
Irony, romantic, 156
Islam, 30, 120
Itinerant philosophers / political theorists, 8, 119f
"It Is Best for Asia to Stand Interdependently," 49

Japan: Zhang Binglin and, 17–43 *passim*, 49, 56f, 66f, 73–83 *passim*, 101, 114, 121, 152–57 *passim*; overseas Chinese in (except Zhang Binglin), 18–23 *passim*, 28–43, 67, 74, 137; and Manchurian Incident, 21; Sino-Japanese War (1894–95), 28, 48f, 95–96; and Buddhism, 36, 74, 80; Meiji Restoration, 59, 74, 135; and India, 63, 77–83 *passim*; "national learning" in, 72, 164–65; imperialism of, 102; and national religion, 103; Liang Qichao and, 105–6, 107; *bakufu* of, 114, 135; school system in, 134f; socialists and anarchists of, 137–41 *passim*
Jesuits, 93
Ji, 65, 153. *See also* Literature
Jiang Liangqi, 28
Jianlun, 16, 67, 71, 112
Jiao (doctrine), 102–3, 114–15
Jiaozhi, 152
Jiaozhou tongyi, 67
Jiaozhu (religious founder), 114–15
Jia Yi, 53–54
Ji clan, 32
Jie Ni, 130
Jin dynasty, 40f; Wei-Jin, 27; Eastern, 41
Jing, 69f, 153f. *See also* Classical studies
Jingyi shuwen, 47
"Ji Yindu Xipoqi wang jinianhui shi," 76–82
Jiyun, 38
"Jue sheng," 137–38
Jurchens, 41

Kang Youwei, xi, xiv, 49–59 *passim*, 151, 154; Zhang Binglin and, 8, 13, 17ff, 23, 31–32, 49–57 *passim*, 65, 70f, 109, 111, 120ff, 132, 140, 148; and Treaty of Shimonoseki, 48, 95–96; and Confucianism, 53, 95–108, 114f, 122, 132–41 *passim*, 161–69 *passim*; and India, 77; and *zhuzi*, 96–99 *passim*, 116, 120
Kant, Immanuel, 34, 66, 94

Library of Congress Cataloging-in-Publication Data

Shimada, Kenji, 1917–
  [Shō Heirin ni tsuite. English]
  Pioneer of the Chinese revolution : Zhang Binglin and Confucianism
/ Shimada Kenji ; translated by Joshua A. Fogel.
      p.   cm.
  Translation of: Shō Heirin ni tsuite and Shingai Kakumei ki no
Kōshi mondai.
  ISBN 0-8047-1581-5 (alk. paper) :
  1. Chang, T'ai-yen, 1868–1936. 2. China—History—1861–1912.
3. China—History—1912–1928. 4. Nationalism—China—History.
5. Scholars—China—Biography. 6. Confucianism—China—20th
century. I. Shimada, Kenji, 1917– Shingai Kakumei ki no Kōshi
mondai. 1990. II. Title.
CT3990.C485313   1990
951.04′1′092—dc20
[B]   90-30377
                                                          CIP